English Pronunciation in Use

Elementary

Self-study and
classroom use

Jonathan Marks

CAMBRIDGE
UNIVERSITY PRESS

CAMBRIDGE UNIVERSITY PRESS
Cambridge, New York, Melbourne, Madrid, Cape Town, Singapore, São Paulo

CAMBRIDGE UNIVERSITY PRESS
The Edinburgh Building, Cambridge CB2 8RU, UK

www.cambridge.org
Information on this title: www.cambridge.org/9780521672627

© Cambridge University Press 2007

First published 2007

Printed in the United Kingdom at the University Press, Cambridge

A catalogue record for this publication is available from the British Library

ISBN 978-0-521-67262-7 paperback
ISBN 978-0-521-67264-1 audio CDs (5)
ISBN 978-0-521-67266-5 paperback and CDs pack
ISBN 978-0-521-69370-7 CD-ROM
ISBN 978-0-521-69373-8 CD-ROM, paperback and CDs pack

Contents

To the student

The *English Pronunciation in Use Elementary* course – book and CDs, or book and cassettes – is to help you with your English pronunciation.

What will I need?

You will need a cassette or CD player to listen to the recordings. The symbol (A1) shows the track numbers of the recordings. It will be useful if you can record your own voice, so that you can listen to your own pronunciation and hear your progress.

When you are studying individual sounds it is sometimes useful to have a mirror, so that you can see the shape of your mouth and compare it with the diagrams in the book.

How is *English Pronunciation in Use Elementary* organised?

There are 50 two-page units in the book. Each unit is about a different pronunciation point. Section A (Units 1 to 27) is about how to say and spell individual sounds, and groups of sounds together. Section B (Units 28 to 32) is about joining sounds to make words. Section C (Units 33 to 43) is about pronunciation in phrases and sentences. Section D (Units 44 to 50) is about pronunciation in conversation. The left-hand page of each unit has explanations and examples, and the right-hand page has exercises (except Units 49 and 50).

After these units is Section E, where you will find:
E1 Chart of phonemic symbols – with example words for every symbol.
E2 Guide for speakers of specific languages – Speakers of different languages have different problems with English pronunciation, and this guide shows which units in the book may be especially helpful for them.
E3 Sound pairs – If you have problems with hearing the difference between pairs of sounds, you can find extra practice here.
E4 From spelling to sound – In English, the same sound can often be spelled in different ways. Here you will find the most common spellings of each sound.
E5 The alphabet – exercises to help you say the letters of the alphabet, and understand them when you hear them.
E6 Pronouncing numbers – exercises to help you pronounce different kinds of numbers, and understand them when you hear them.
E7 Pronouncing geographical names – how to pronounce the names of countries, continents, etc.
E8 Homophones – words that are spelled differently but sound the same.

Why not have a look at Section E now, before you start the book?

At the end of the book there is a Key with answers to all the exercises.

The CDs or cassettes contain all the recordings for the left- and right-hand pages of the units, and Section E.

How should I use the course?

You can simply study the units from 1 to 50, or you can alternate units from different sections. For example, you could do Unit 1, then Unit 28, then Unit 33, then Unit 44, then Unit 2, and so on.

If you want to focus your work more closely, you can look at the *Guide for speakers of specific languages* in Section E2. This tells you which units are most important for speakers of different languages.

In Section A, if you have problems hearing the difference between individual sounds, go to the *Sound pair* indicated (in Section E3).

When you are working with the recordings, you should replay a track as often as you need to. When you are doing an exercise you may also need to pause the recording after each sentence to give yourself time to think or write your answer. When you are asked to repeat single words, there is a space on the recording for you to do this, but when you are repeating whole sentences you will need to pause the recording to give yourself enough time to repeat.

Will *English Pronunciation in Use Elementary* only help me with my speaking? What about listening?

Pronunciation is important for both speaking and listening, and this course will also help you with your listening. Some pronunciation points are especially important for listening, and these are indicated like this:

What type of English pronunciation is used in *English Pronunciation in Use Elementary*?

As a model for you to copy when you speak, we have used only one type of pronunciation, a standard British type. But in the listening exercises you will hear a wider variety of accents, including some non-native speakers.

Recordings

CD A: Units 1–12
CD B: Units 13–27
CD C: Units 28–43
CD D: Units 44–50, Sections E1, E4–E8
CD E: Section E3 Sound pairs

To the teacher

English Pronunciation in Use Elementary has been written so that it can be used for self-study, but it will work equally well in the classroom. The advantages of working on pronunciation in the classroom include the following points.

- Learners can get guidance and immediate feedback from the teacher.
- Learners can practise the dialogues and other exercises in pairs.
- You can direct learners with particular pronunciation difficulties to do specific units on their own or in small groups, if appropriate.

In order to make the material accessible to learners, terminology has been kept as simple as possible. The remainder of this Introduction describes how the course is organised, and it is followed by a *Map of the contents* using standard terminology.

English Pronunciation in Use Elementary progresses from individual sounds, through sequences of sounds, and stress in words, to intonation patterns in phrases and sentences. Of course, as soon as learners begin to speak English, they need to begin to develop control of all these features in parallel, but the step-by-step, incremental approach adopted here is designed to facilitate a clear progression and a clear focus on one thing at a time. Nevertheless, learners do not necessarily have to work their way through all the units in each section in sequence; they can alternate units from different sections.

Section A Sounds and spelling

Unit 1 deals with some general issues of pronunciation and spelling. Units 2 to 23 introduce the phonemes (sounds) of English, first the vowels and then the consonants. Generally, two sounds are introduced in each unit, though some units have one or three. They are paired on the basis of similarity of spelling, similarity of articulation and potential for confusion. Guidance is given as to the most frequent spellings of each phoneme, and practice is given in some significant contrasts between phonemes.

One phoneme not specifically focused on in Section A is the weak vowel /ə/, the *schwa*; the emphasis is on pronouncing vowel sounds (and consonants, too) in stressed syllables, where accuracy and clarity are most important, and the *schwa* is treated as a feature of unstressed syllables rather than a sound with the same status as the other vowel phonemes.

Units 24 to 27 deal with consonant clusters.

Section B Syllables and words

Section B introduces the concept of syllables, the distinction between strong and weak syllables, and stress patterns in words.

Section C Phrases, sentences and grammar

Section C moves the focus from individual words to phrases and sentences, and highlights links between pronunciation and various aspects of grammar which are learned at elementary level.

Section D Conversation

Finally, Section D deals with aspects of intonation in the context of sentences and longer stretches of language such as dialogues, stories and conversation. It also covers some characteristic intonation patterns of common lexical phrases.

Intonation is very variable, and the intonation patterns attached to phrases and grammatical structures in these units are certainly not the only ones possible. However, they are very commonly – characteristically, even – used in these contexts, and the associations between intonation and contexts should help to make the intonation patterns memorable.

Section E Reference

Section E contains various kinds of further reference and practice material. The *Guide for speakers of specific languages* and *Sound pairs* can be used to prioritise certain pronunciation points and to reject others, depending on learners' particular needs.

What model of pronunciation?

As a model for learners to copy when they speak, I have used a standard southern British accent. This can be regarded as a provisional target, but learners will vary as to how closely they will want or need to achieve it. Some features of pronunciation are important for listening, but less essential for learners to imitate, and these are labelled as such. Nevertheless, attempting to reproduce these features should help learners in their ability to understand speech which contains them, and they may want to make the effort of incorporating them in their own English. In the listening exercises, a wider variety of accents can be heard, including some non-native speakers; it is important that learners at this level begin to get exposure to a variety of accents.

Recordings

CD A: Units 1–12
CD B: Units 13–27
CD C: Units 28–43
CD D: Units 44–50, Sections E1, E4–E8
CD E: Section E3 Sound pairs

Map of contents

1 How many letters, how many sounds?
Spelling and pronunciation

A

All sections with this symbol 🎧 are on the recording. Listen to them while you read this page.

(A2a) There are **26 letters** in the English alphabet.
A B C D E F G H I J K L M N O P Q R S T U V W X Y Z

(A2b) There are five **vowel** letters. A E I O U

(A2c) And there are 21 **consonant** letters. B C D F G H J K L M N P Q R S T V W X Y Z

(A2d) But there are more than 40 vowel and consonant **sounds** in English.
In some words, the number of letters is the same as the number of sounds.

best   4 letters, 4 sounds

b	e	s	t
1	2	3	4

dentist   7 letters, 7 sounds

d	e	n	t	i	s	t
1	2	3	4	5	6	7

B

But sometimes the number of sounds is different from the number of letters.

(A3a) In **green**, ee is one sound, and in **happy**, pp is one sound.

green   5 letters, 4 sounds

g	r	e	e	n		h	a	p	p	y
1	2	3		4		1	2	3		4

(A3b) In **bread**, ea is one sound.
bread   5 letters, 4 sounds

b	r	e	a	d
1	2	3		4

(A3c) In some words there are silent letters (letters with no sound). In **listen**, t is silent.
listen   6 letters, 5 sounds.

l	i	s	t	e	n
1	2	3	-	4	5

(A3d) In some words, one letter is two sounds. The **x** in **six** is two sounds like **k + s**.
six   3 letters, 4 sounds

s	i	x	
1	2	3	4

C

We sometimes write the same sound differently in different words. For example, the e in **red** sounds like the **ea** in **bread**.

(A4a) Sometimes two words have the same pronunciation but different spellings. (See Section E8 *Homophones*.)
know – no
A: Do you **know**? B: **No**, I don't.

(A4b) And sometimes two words have the same spelling but different pronunciations.
read (infinitive and present tense) – read (past tense)
A: Do you want to **read** the newspaper?
B: No, thanks, I **read** it this morning.

(A4c) Because there are more sounds than letters, we use symbols for pronunciation.

/best/ best   /ˈdentɪst/ dentist   /griːn/ green   /ˈhæpi/ happy   /ˈkɒfi/ coffee   /ˈlɪsən/ listen
/θriː/ three   /sɪks/ six   /sɒks/ socks   /bred/ bread   /nəʊ/ no   /nəʊ/ know   /red/ red
/red/ read (past tense)   /riːd/ read (infinitive and present tense)

The symbol ˈ (look at the beginning of the symbols for *dentist, happy, coffee, listen*) comes before stressed syllables (see Section B *Syllables and words*).

Exercises

1.1 Write the number of letters and the number of sounds in these words.

	letters	sounds
green	5	4
1 all		
2 back		
3 could		
4 knee		
5 sixty		
6 thing		
7 who		
8 address		

(A5) Check with the Key (on page 138). Then listen and repeat.

1.2 Some pronunciation symbols are easy. Write these words in their normal spelling.

EXAMPLE /best/ ....*best*........
1 /bɪg/ .... 2 /dres/ .... 3 /frend/ .... 4 /gɪv/ ....
5 /help/ .... 6 /nekst/ .... 7 /'veri/ .... 8 /wel/ ....

(A6) Check with the Key. Then listen and repeat.

1.3 All five words in each group have the same vowel letter – a, e, i, o or u – but one has a different vowel sound. Circle the word with the different vowel sound in each group.

EXAMPLE
on	top	stop	(one)	gone
1 give	time	sit	think	rich
2 apple	bad	wash	catch	bank
3 much	bus	sun	push	up
4 many	maths	man	hat	flat

(A7) Check with the Key. Then listen and repeat.

1.4 Write words that **rhyme** (the end part of the word sounds the same).

EXAMPLE
red   b<u>e</u> <u>d</u>
1 key   tr_ _
2 blue   sh_ _
3 not   w_ _ _
4 one   r_ _
5 date   w_ _ _
6 lie   w_ _
7 so   sh_ _
8 beer   n_ _ _

(A8) Check with the Key. Then listen and repeat.

2 Pizza for dinner
/iː/ and /ɪ/

A · How to make the sound /iː/

A9a · /iː/ is a long sound. Look at the diagram. Listen and then say the sound. Make your mouth wide, like a smile. Your tongue touches the sides of your teeth. Target sound: /iː/

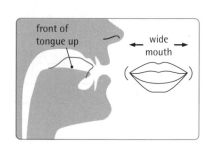

front of tongue up   ← wide mouth →

B · Sound and spelling

A9b · /iː/ is usually spelled ee or ea. Listen and say these words.
   see   agree   eat   seat   team

A9c · Listen and say these other words with /iː/.
   ie   field   piece
   e   these   metre   secret   evening   equal   Peter   museum   European   Chinese
        Japanese   complete
   ey   key
   i   ski   kilo   litre   pizza   police   machine   magazine
   eo   people

A9d · Now listen and say these sentences. You will need to pause the recording to give yourself enough time to repeat.
   1 Can you see the sea?
   2 A piece of pizza, please.
   3 Peter's in the team.
   4 A kilo of peaches and a litre of cream.
   5 Please can you teach me to speak Portuguese?

Can you see the sea?

C · How to make the sound /ɪ/

A10a · /ɪ/ is a short sound. Look at the diagram. Listen and then say the sound. Make your mouth a bit less wide than for /iː/. Your tongue is a bit further back in your mouth than for /iː/. Target sound: /ɪ/

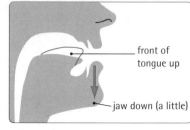

front of tongue up

jaw down (a little)

D · Sound and spelling

A10b · /ɪ/ is usually spelled i. Listen and say these words.
   if   listen   miss   dinner   swim

A10c · Listen and say these other words with /ɪ/.
   busy   business   building   system

A10d · Now listen and say these phrases.
   1 fifty-six
   2 dinner in the kitchen
   3 a cinema ticket
   4 a picture of a building
   5 big business

A10e · Note: Eight letters of the alphabet have the sound /iː/. Listen and repeat.
   B C D E G P T V

A10f · Note: Units 2 to 10 focus on vowel sounds in stressed syllables (see Section B *Syllables and words*).
 Vowel sounds in unstressed syllables often have the weak vowel /ə/. Listen and repeat.
   agree   equal   kitchen   museum   Peter   picture   pizza

A10g · Note: There is sometimes an /i/ sound at the end of a word in an unstressed syllable (see Section B *Syllables and words*), e.g. happy, coffee, busy. This sound is like /iː/ but shorter. Listen and repeat.
   happy   coffee   busy   sixty

Exercises

2.1 Put these /iː/ words in the dialogues.

email	evening	police	~~secret~~	Steve	TV

1 A: What shall we do this ....?
B: Let's stay at home and watch ....
2 A: Let me read that ....
B: No – it's a .... *secret* .... !
3 A: You know my friend ....?
B: Yes.
A: Well, he's got a new job. He's joined the ....!

(A11) Listen to check your answers. Check with the Key. Then listen and repeat.

What shall we do?

2.2 Find the /ɪ/ words from these clues.

EXAMPLE A thousand thousand is a .... *million* ....
1 You can use a .... to go up and down in a building.
2 There are sixty seconds in a ....
3 A .... is a book of words to help you with your English.
4 It's too warm in here – open the ....
5 Would you like a .... with your coffee?
6 Birds and planes have ....
7 You can see yourself in a ....
8 Don't drop .... – put it in a bin!

1,000,000 ✓

DICTIONARY

(A12) Listen to check your answers. Check with the Key.
Then listen and repeat.

2.3 Circle all the /iː/ sounds and underline all the /ɪ/ sounds.

big	busy	dinner	give	green	in	listen	meet	office	people	pizza
please	repeat	six	tea	three						

(A13) Listen to check your answers. Then listen and repeat.

2.4 Match the beginnings and endings of the sentences.

EXAMPLE Let's have pizza .... *for dinner* ....
1 We're always busy ....
2 Would you like tea ....
3 Give me that big ....
4 There were only three ....
5 Listen and ....
6 Let's meet at ....

a repeat.
b people in the museum.
c six o'clock.
d in the office.
e or coffee?
f green book, please.
g ~~for dinner.~~

(A14) Check with the Key. Then listen and repeat.

2.5 Listen and circle the word you hear. Check with the Key. If any of these are difficult for you, go to Section E3 *Sound pairs* for further practice.

(A15)
1 *leave / live*   (⇒ sound pair 1)
2 *knee / near*   (⇒ sound pair 2)
3 *litter / letter*   (⇒ sound pair 3)

3 A spoonful of sugar
/uː/ and /ʊ/

A

How to make the sound /uː/

 • /uː/ is a long sound. Look at the diagram. Listen and then say the sound. Make your lips into a tunnel shape. Your tongue is a long way back in your mouth. Target sound: /uː/

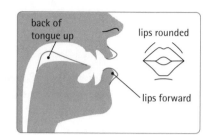

back of tongue up

lips rounded

lips forward

B

Sound and spelling

 • /uː/ is often spelled **oo**, **ou**, **oe**, **u**, **ue** or **ew**. Listen and say these words.

too   group   shoe   blue

 • When the spelling is **u** or **ew**, there is often a /j/ sound before the /uː/. Listen and say these words.

music   new

 • There are also other spellings of /uː/. Listen and say these other words with /uː/.

two   fruit   juice

 • Now listen and say these phrases.

1 me too
2 work in groups
3 new shoes
4 red and blue
5 listen to the music
6 forty-two
7 fruit juice

⚠ Note: /juː/ is the name of the letter U in the alphabet.

C

How to make the sound /ʊ/

 • /ʊ/ is a short sound. Look at the diagram. Listen and then say the sound. Your tongue is not so far back as for /uː/. Target sound: /ʊ/

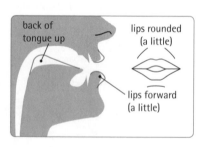

back of tongue up

lips rounded (a little)

lips forward (a little)

D

Sound and spelling

 • /ʊ/ is often spelled **u**, **oo** or **ou**. Listen and say these words.

full   sugar   book   foot   would

 • Listen and say this other word with /ʊ/.

woman

 • Now listen and say these phrases.

1 My bag's full.
2 Where's my book?
3 my left foot
4 a kilo of sugar
5 Who's that woman?

Exercises

3.1 Circle the words with /uː/. (There are nine.)

(food) four June look news room school soup spoon sugar town Tuesday two

A18 Listen to check your answers. Check with the Key. Then listen and repeat.

3.2 Put the /uː/ words from Exercise 3.1 in the sentences.
1 Do you like fast ....food........ ?
2 Are you coming to ....?
3 It's .... the second of ....
4 Let's watch the ....
5 .... is over there.
6 Here's a .... for your ....

A19 Listen to check your answers. Check with the Key. Then listen and repeat.

3.3 Circle the words with /ʊ/. (There are six.)

(book) cookery cough could good looking lunch soon sugar thought through

A20 Listen to check your answers. Check with the Key. Then listen and repeat.

3.4 Put the /ʊ/ words from Exercise 3.3 in the sentences.
1 Do you take ....?
2 .... you help me? I'm .... for a ....cookery........ ....

A21 Listen to check your answers. Check with the Key. Then listen and repeat.

3.5 Circle the words that have /uː/ or /ʊ/, then put them in the correct column.

1 Is it really (true)?
2 You're standing on my (foot)!
3 Are you a good cook?
4 Where's my toothbrush?
5 Do you push or pull to open this door?
6 I'll be ready soon.
7 Here's your ticket – don't lose it!
8 Go through that door over there.
9 My keys! Where did I put them?

/uː/	/ʊ/
true	foot

A22 Listen to check your answers. Check with the Key. Then listen and repeat.

3.6 Listen and circle the word you hear. Check with the Key. If any of these are difficult for you, go to Section E3 *Sound pairs* for further practice.

A23 1 *pool / pull*   (⇒ sound pair 4)
    2 *look / luck*   (⇒ sound pair 5)
    3 *soup / soap*   (⇒ sound pair 6)

4 Father and mother
/ɑː/ and /ʌ/

A

How to make the sound /ɑː/

- /ɑː/ is a long sound. Look at the diagram. Listen and then say the sound. Open your mouth wide. Target sound: /ɑː/

back of tongue down

jaw down (a little)

B

Sound and spelling

- /ɑː/ is usually spelled a or ar. Listen and say these words.

after afternoon ask answer bath bathroom can't class dance fast
father glass tomato bar car card far park star start

- Listen and say these other words with /ɑː/.

aunt laugh heart half (The letter l in **half** is silent.)

- Listen and say these sentences.
  1 How far's the car park?
  2 We went to a large bar full of film stars.
  3 We're starting in half an hour.

- In words with a letter **r** after the /ɑː/ sound, most Americans and some British people pronounce the r. Listen to the same sentences, this time with the letter **r**s pronounced.

 Important for listening

- Some people, especially in the north of England, pronounce the letters **a** or **au** as /æ/ in some of these words. Listen.

after afternoon ask answer aunt bath bathroom class dance fast glass laugh

Listen to these sentences, first with /ɑː/, then with /æ/.
  1 See you tomorrow afternoon.   3 We were laughing and dancing in the classroom.
  2 I'll ask my aunt.   4 I left my glasses in the bathroom.

⚠️ Note: The name of the letter R is pronounced /ɑː/ or /ɑːr/.
⚠️ Note: The word *are* is often pronounced /ɑː/ or /ɑːr/. (See Unit 40.)

C

How to make the sound /ʌ/

- /ʌ/ is a short sound. Look at the diagram. Listen and then say the sound. Open your mouth wide. Target sound: /ʌ/

tongue down

relaxed lips

relaxed jaw

D

Sound and spelling

- /ʌ/ is usually spelled u, but sometimes ou or o. Listen and say these words.

bus colour come cup front London luck Monday month mother
much nothing number run study sun uncle under

⚠️ Note: The words *son* and *sun* have the same pronunciation.
⚠️ Note: The number *one* is pronounced /wʌn/.

- Listen and say these sentences.
  1 Good luck with your exam next month!
  2 Take the number one bus.
  3 I said 'Come on Monday', not 'Come on Sunday'.
  4 My brother's studying in London.

 Important for listening

Some people, especially in the north of England, say /ʊ/ instead of /ʌ/. Listen to the same sentences, this time with /ʊ/.

Exercises

4.1 Listen and write the words in the correct column.

(A26)

~~artist~~ garden March part ~~square~~ talk warm watch

words with /ɑː/   **words with other vowel sounds**
  artist   _square_

....

....

....

Check with the Key. Then listen again and repeat.

4.2 Listen and write the words in the correct column.

(A27)

~~business~~ ~~country~~ fun home lots money mother push

words with /ʌ/   **words with other vowel sounds**
  country   _business_

....

....

....

Check with the Key. Then listen again and repeat.

4.3 Complete the sentences with one /ɑː/ word and one /ʌ/ word.

~~butter~~ carpet dark hard husband love Prague son

1 The ___butter's___ too ....
2 I'd .... to buy that ....!
3 Their ....'s got .... hair.
4 I first met my .... in ....

(A28) Listen to check your answers. Check with the Key. Then listen again and repeat.

4.4 Listen and circle the word you hear. Check with the Key. If any of these are difficult for you, go to Section E3 *Sound pairs* for more practice.

(A29)
1 *heart / hat*   (⇒ sound pair 7)
2 *far / four*   (⇒ sound pair 8)
3 *cat /cut*   (⇒ sound pair 9)
4 *look / luck*   (⇒ sound pair 5)
5 *luck / lock*   (⇒ sound pair 10)
6 *butter / better*   (⇒ sound pair 18)

5 A dog in the corner
/ɒ/ and /ɔː/

A

How to make the sound /ɒ/

A30a
- /ɒ/ is a short sound. Look at the diagram. Listen and say the sound. Round your lips a little. The front of your tongue is low and towards the back of your mouth. Target sound: /ɒ/

front of tongue down · lips rounded (a little) · lips forward · jaw down

B

Sound and spelling

A30b
- /ɒ/ is usually spelled o, and sometimes a. Listen and repeat.

bottle	box	chocolate	clock	coffee	copy	cost	cross	doctor	dog	gone
got	holiday	hospital	hot	job	lock	long	lost	lot	not	off	often
possible	shop	song	sorry	stop	top	wrong				
quality	want	wash	wasn't	watch	what					

⚠ Note: The word *cough* is pronounced /kɒf/.
Note: The word *was* is sometimes pronounced with /ɒ/. (See Unit 40.)

A30c
- Now listen and say these sentences.
  1 Have you got a lot of shopping?
  2 John's gone to the shops.
  3 How much did your holiday cost?
  4 She said the coffee wasn't very good, but I thought it was.

A30d

Important for listening

Most Americans pronounce these words differently. Listen.

1 Have you got a lot of shopping?
2 John's gone to the shops.
3 How much did your holiday cost?
4 She said the coffee wasn't very good, but I thought it was.

C

How to make the sound /ɔː/

front of tongue down · lips very rounded · lips foward · jaw down

A31a
- /ɔː/ is a long sound. Look at the diagram. Listen and say the sound. Round your lips more than for /ɒ/. Target sound: /ɔː/

D

Sound and spelling

A31b
- /ɔː/ has different spellings. Listen and say these words.

a	all	ball	call	fall	tall	ar	quarter	warm	
	wall	water				or	born	corner	forty	horse
al	talk	walk					short	sort	
au	autumn					oor	door	floor	
aw	saw					ore	before	more	
augh	caught	daughter	taught			our	four		
ough	bought	thought							

A31c
- Now listen and say these phrases.
  1 quarter past four
  2 born in autumn
  3 have some more
  4 walking on water
  5 the fourth door on the fourth floor

A31d

Important for listening

When there is a letter r after /ɔː/, most Americans, Scots and Irish, and some other English speakers pronounce this r. Listen.

1 quarter past four
2 born in autumn
3 have some more
4 walking on water
5 the fourth door on the fourth floor

Exercises

5.1 Write these words.

EXAMPLE /bɒks/ .... *box* ....
1 /klɒk/ ....
2 /gɒn/ ....
3 /wɒnt/ ....
4 /'wɒntɪd/ ....
5 /'sɒri/ ....
6 /wɒt/ ....

(A32) Listen to check your answers. Check with the Key. Then listen again and repeat.

5.2 Listen and complete the dialogues with these /ɒ/ words.

(A33)

| box | chocolates | clock | doctor | gone | got | holiday | on | stopped |

~~what~~ what

1 A: .... *What* .... time is it?
   B: I don't know. The ....'s ....
2 A: .... have you ....?
   B: A .... of ....
3 A: Where's the ....?
   B: He's ....

Check with the Key. Then listen again and repeat.

What time is it?

5.3 Write the underlined verbs in the past tense.

EXAMPLE
We <u>buy</u> everything at the supermarket. → We ...... *bought* ...... everything at the supermarket.
1 I <u>think</u> about you every day. → I .... about you every day.
2 We always <u>walk</u> home from school. → We always .... home from school.
3 I <u>catch</u> the first bus in the morning. → I .... the first bus in the morning.
4 My daughter <u>teaches</u> English. → My daughter .... English.

(A34) Check with the Key. Then listen and repeat.

5.4 Write the names of the things in the picture.
(They all have /ɒ/ or /ɔː/.)

EXAMPLE ...... 1 *bottle* ......

Check with the Key.

5.5 Listen and write the missing /ɒ/ and /ɔː/ words.

(A35) This is our kitchen. On the table there's a big .... full of shopping, a .... of wine and some .... and pepper. There's a .... on the .... and the .... 's asleep in the corner behind the ....

Check with the Key. Then listen and speak together with the recording.

5.6 Listen and circle the word you hear. Check with the Key. If any of these are difficult for you, go to Section E3 *Sound pairs* for more practice.

(A36)
1 *not / note* (⇒ sound pair 11)
2 *luck / lock* (⇒ sound pair 10)
3 *coat / caught* (⇒ sound pair 12)
4 *shot / short* (⇒ sound pair 13)
5 *walk / work* (⇒ sound pair 14)

6 Bread and jam
/e/ and /æ/

A How to make the sound /e/

A37a • /e/ is a short sound. Look at the diagram. Listen and say the sound. Open your mouth quite wide. Target sound: /e/

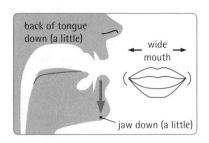

back of tongue down (a little)
wide mouth
jaw down (a little)

B Sound and spelling

A37b • /e/ is usually spelled e, but sometimes **ea**, **ie**, **a** or **ai**. Listen and repeat.

e	check	leg	letter	red	sentence
ea	bread	head	read (past tense)		
ie	friend				
a	any	many			
ai	again	said			

A37c • Listen and say these sentences.

1 Tell me again.
2 Send me a cheque.
3 Correct these sentences.
4 Twenty to twelve.
5 Help your friend.

C How to make the sound /æ/

A38a • /æ/ is a short sound. Look at the diagram. Listen and say the sound. Open your mouth wide. Target sound: /æ/

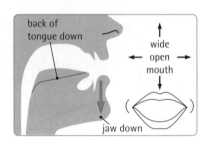

back of tongue down
wide open mouth
jaw down

D Sound and spelling

A38b • /æ/ is usually spelled **a**. Listen and repeat.

back   camera   factory   hat   jam   manager   map   plan   traffic

A38c • Listen and say these sentences.

1 Thanks for the cash.
2 I ran to the bank.
3 Where's my black jacket?
4 That man works in a jam factory.
5 Let me carry your bags.

Exercises

6.1 Write these words.

EXAMPLE /mæp/ ....map........

1 /hænd/ ....
2 /best/ ....
3 /eg/ ....
4 /mæn/ ....

5 /men/ ....
6 /'meni/ ....
7 /hæv/ ....
8 /nekst/ ....

(A39) Check with the Key. Then listen and repeat.

6.2 Seven of these numbers have /e/. Which are they?

3   7 ✓   8   10   11   12   13   17   18   20   70   80   100
    seven   ....

(A40) Check with the Key. Then listen and repeat.

6.3 Match the phrases to make sentences with an /æ/ and an /e/.

The first plan was the best.

1 The first plan ......was the best...... .
2 He said ....
3 How many ....
4 I haven't got ....
5 I'll be back ....
6 My friends live ....

a any milk.
b again tomorrow.
c in a flat over there.
d stamps do you need?
e ~~was the best.~~
f 'Thank you.'

(A41) Check with the Key. Then listen and repeat.

6.4 Listen and circle the word you hear. Check with the Key. If any of these are difficult for you, go to Section E3 *Sound pairs* for more practice.

(A42) 1 *men / man*   (⇒ sound pair 15)
2 *cat / cut*   (⇒ sound pair 9)
3 *had / hard*   (⇒ sound pair 7)
4 *pepper / paper*   (⇒ sound pair 16)
5 *head / heard*   (⇒ sound pair 17)
6 *set / sit*   (⇒ sound pair 3)
7 *better / butter*   (⇒ sound pair 18)

7 My birthday's on Thursday
/ɜː/

A

How to make the sound /ɜː/

A43a • /ɜː/ is a long sound. Look at the diagram. Listen and say
the sound. To make this sound, your mouth and your
tongue should be very relaxed. Target sound: /ɜː/

relaxed lips,
tongue and jaw

⚠ Note: /ɜː/ is a sound English speakers often make when they
A43b aren't sure what to say, and we often write it 'er'. Listen.

A: What date is it today?
B: Er, I think it's the tenth.

B

Sound and spelling

A43c • /ɜː/ is spelled **ir**, **or**, **ur**, **our**, **ear** or **er**. Listen and say these words.

ir	bird	first	birthday	circle	thirty
or	word	work	world	worse	worst
ur	turn	Thursday			
our	journey				
ear	early	earth	heard	learn	
er	service	Germany	prefer	dessert	weren't	verb	university

⚠ Note: The words *her*, *hers* and *were* are often pronounced with /ɜː/. (See Units 38 and 40.)

A43d • Now listen and say these sentences.

My birthday's on Thursday the
thirty-first and hers is a week later.

1 My birthday's on Thursday the thirty-first, and hers is a week later.
2 When would you prefer, Tuesday or Thursday?
3 That was the worst journey in the world!
4 Have you ever heard this word?
5 A: The cakes weren't very good.
   B: I thought they were.
6 She went to university to learn German.

A43e

Important for listening

Notice that there's always an r in the spelling of /ɜː/. Most Americans, Scots and Irish, and some other
English speakers pronounce these rs (see Unit 22). Listen.

1 My birthday's on Thursday the thirty-first, and hers is a week later.
2 When would you prefer, Tuesday or Thursday?
3 That was the worst journey in the world!
4 Have you ever heard this word?
5 A: The cakes weren't very good.
   B: I thought they were.
6 She went to university to learn German.

Exercises

7.1 Listen and put the words in the correct groups.

(A44)

~~beard~~	~~ear~~	chair	~~church~~	curtains	dirty	~~door~~	floor	four	girl	horse
large	March	near	nurse	pair	parked	purse	shirt	shorts	stars	surfer
third	warm	wearing								

words with /ɜ:/
1 ...*church*...
2 ....
3 ....
4 ....
5 ....
6 ....
7 ....
8 ....
9 ....

words with /ɔ:/
1 ...*door*...
2 ....
3 ....
4 ....
5 ....
6 ....

words with /ɑ:/
1 ...*car*...
2 ....
3 ....
4 ....
5 ....

words with other sounds
1 ...*beard*...
2 ....
3 ....
4 ....
5 ....

Check with the Key. Then listen again and repeat.

7.2 Look at the picture and complete the sentences, using the words from Exercise 7.1.

1 The ...*nurse*... is sitting on a .... next to the ....
2 The boy's .... a .... of .... and a ....
3 There's a man with a .... standing .... the ....
4 The girl's .... is on the .... next to the bed.
5 It's .... in the room.
6 The date is the .... of ....
7 There's a picture of a ...., and a picture of ....
8 There are flowers on the ....
9 Through the windows, you can see a ...., with a .... outside. There are some .... in the sky.

(A45) Listen to check your answers. Check with the Key. Then listen again and repeat.

7.3 Listen and write the numbers you hear.

(A46) EXAMPLE ...*42*...

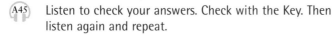

1 ....   3 ....   5 ....   7 ....
2 ....   4 ....   6 ....   8 ....

Check with the Key. Then listen again and repeat.

7.4 Listen and circle the word you hear. Check with the Key. If you find any of these difficult, go to Section E3 *Sound pairs* for further practice.

(A47)
1 *shirts / shorts*   (⇒ sound pair 14)   3 *bird / beard*   (⇒ sound pair 20)
2 *first / fast*   (⇒ sound pair 19)   4 *heard / head*   (⇒ sound pair 17)

8 Here and there
/ɪə/ and /eə/

A   How to make the sound /ɪə/

 • /ɪə/ is a long sound. It moves from /ɪ/ to /ə/. Look at the diagram. Listen and say the sound. Target sound: /ɪə/

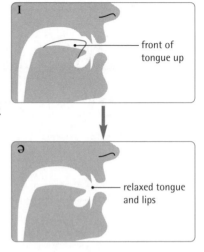

I — front of tongue up

ə — relaxed tongue and lips

⚠ Note: When you say the sound /ɪə/ by itself, you say the word *ear*.

B   Sound and spelling

 • /ɪə/ is spelled in different ways. Listen and repeat.

ea	real					
ear	ear	beard	clear	hear	nearly	year
eer	beer	cheers				
ere	here	we're				

 • Listen and say these sentences.

1 We're here!
2 Have a beer – cheers!
3 Is there a bank near here?
4 The meaning isn't really clear.

C   How to make the sound /eə/

 • /eə/ is a long sound. It moves from /e/ to /ə/. Look at the diagram. Listen and say the sound. Target sound: /eə/

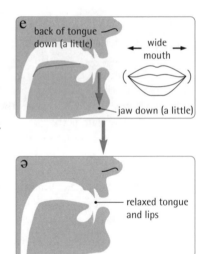

e — back of tongue down (a little) — wide mouth — jaw down (a little)

ə — relaxed tongue and lips

⚠ Note: When you say the sound /eə/ by itself, you say the word *air*.

D   Sound and spelling

 • /eə/ is spelled in different ways. Listen and repeat.

are	care	square			
air	air	chair	fair	hair	stair
ear	wear				
ere	where				
aer	aeroplane				

 • Listen and say these sentences.

A: Look at that aeroplane!
B: Where?
A: Up there, in the air, of course!

 Sometimes you hear an /r/ sound after /ɪə/ or /eə/. Listen.

Important for listening

with /r/	ear	nearly	air	where
without /r/	ear	nearly	air	where

Exercises

8.1 Read this note and find four /ɪə/ words and four /eə/ words.

> Dear Mary,
>
> I'm really pleased you can come to the theatre with us tonight.
>
> We've got seats upstairs, near the front. See you there!
>
> Sarah

/ɪə/   1 Dear _____   2 _____   3 _____   4 _____
/eə/   1 Mary _____   2 _____   3 _____   4 _____

(A50) Listen to check your answers. Check with the Key. Then listen and repeat.

8.2 Complete these sentences with /ɪə/ and /eə/ words.

1 She's got __fair__ h_____ .
2 The ch_____ are under the st_____ .
3 How many y_____ have you lived h_____ ?
4 There's a man with a b_____ sitting in the s_____ .
5 Speak up! I can't h_____ you.
6 It's a cl_____ day – you can see for miles.

(A51) Listen to check your answers. Check with the Key. Then listen and repeat.

8.3 Listen. Can you hear an /r/ sound after the /ɪə/ or /eə/ in the underlined words? Circle the correct
(A52) answer.

EXAMPLE
   See you next <u>year</u>.   /r/   (no /r/)
1 See you next <u>year</u>.   /r/   no /r/
2 <u>We're</u> from England – what about you?   /r/   no /r/
3 Bye – take <u>care</u>!   /r/   no /r/
4 Bye – take <u>care</u>!   /r/   no /r/
5 <u>Where</u> shall we meet?   /r/   no /r/
6 <u>Where</u> shall we meet?   /r/   no /r/

Check with the Key.

8.4 Listen and repeat these poems.
(A53a)
I've had these ears
a hundred years.
Well, no, not really
but very, very nearly!

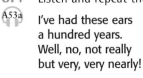

(A53b) When nobody's there
I don't care what I wear,
and I sit on the stair
with my feet on a chair.

8.5 Listen and circle the word you hear. Check with the Key. If any of these are difficult for you, go to
Section E3 *Sound pairs* for further practice.

(A54) 1 *near* / *knee*   (⇒ sound pair 2)
       2 *bird* / *beard*   (⇒ sound pair 20)
       3 *wear* / *way*   (⇒ sound pair 21)

9 Have a great time!
/eɪ/, /aɪ/ and /ɔɪ/

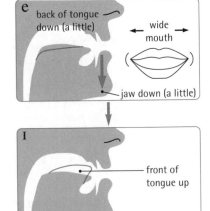

A

How to make the sound /eɪ/

 • /eɪ/ is a long sound. It moves from /e/ to /ɪ/. Look at the diagram. Listen and say the sound. Target sound: /eɪ/

⚠ Note: When you say the sound /eɪ/ by itself, you say the letter A.

B

Sound and spelling

 • /eɪ/ is spelled in different ways. Listen and repeat.

a	age	came	plane	table
ai	rain	wait		
ay	day	play	say	
ey	grey			
ea	break	great		
eigh	eight	weight		

 • Listen and say these sentences.
1 They came a day later.
2 It was a grey day in May.
3 Is this the way to the station?
4 Wait at the gate – I'll be there at **eigh**t.

C

How to make the sound /aɪ/

 • /aɪ/ is a long sound. It moves from /a/ to /ɪ/. Look at the diagram. Listen and say the sound. Target sound: /aɪ/

⚠ Note: When you say the sound /aɪ/ by itself, you say the word *I* or *eye*, or the letter I.

D

Sound and spelling

 • /aɪ/ is spelled in different ways. Listen and repeat.

i	like	time	white
ie	die		
y	dry	July	why
igh	high	night	right
uy	buy		

 • Listen and say these sentences.
1 Do you like dry wine?
2 Why don't you try?
3 July will be fine.
4 Drive on the right.

E

How to make the sound /ɔɪ/

 • /ɔɪ/ is a long sound. It moves from /ɔ/ to /ɪ/. Look at the diagram. Listen and say the sound. Target sound: /ɔɪ/

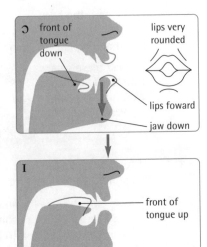

F

Sound and spelling

 • /ɔɪ/ is usually spelled **oi** or **oy**. Listen and repeat.

oi	coin	point	voice
oy	boy	enjoy	toy

 • Listen and say these sentences.
1 I can hear a boy's voice.
2 Those are coins, not toys!

Exercises

9.1 Complete the titles of these pictures.
All the missing words have /eɪ/.

EXAMPLE Ch..*ang*..ing the d..*ate*..
1 W................ing for the tr................
2 T................ing a br................
3 R................ing in Sp................
4 M................ing a m................
5 B................ing a c................

(A58) Listen to check your answers. Check with the Key. Then listen and repeat.

9.2 These verbs are in the past tense. Write the infinitive. They all have /aɪ/.

EXAMPLE drove ....*drive*........
1 wrote .... 3 found .... 5 flew ....
2 tried .... 4 bought ....

(A59) Listen to check your answers. Check with the Key. Then listen and repeat.

9.3 Complete these sentences. All the missing words have /eɪ/ or /aɪ/.

| bye day dry eight flight great miles ~~night~~ right time way white wine |

1 The plane left in the evening and arrived the next morning. It was a ....*night*.................... .
2 It's best to drink .... with fish.
3 Fourteen kilometres is about ....
4 There was no rain yesterday. It was a ....
5 I think I'm lost – is this the .... to the beach?
6 We've had a .... , thanks. .... !

(A60) Listen to check your answers. Check with the Key. Then listen and repeat.

9.4 Look at the pictures and find six things with /eɪ/, three things with /aɪ/ and three things with /ɔɪ/.

/eɪ/ 1 ....*radio*.... 2 t................ 3 c................ 4 t................ 5 p................ 6 s................
/aɪ/ 7 l................ 8 w................ 9 i................
/ɔɪ/ 10 b................ 11 c................ 12 t................

(A61) Listen to check your answers. Check with the Key. Then listen and repeat.

9.5 Listen and circle the word you hear. Check with the Key. If any of these are difficult for you, go to Section E3 *Sound pairs* for further practice.

(A62) 1 *gate / get*   (⇒ sound pair 16)
2 *way / wear*   (⇒ sound pair 21)
3 *my / May*   (⇒ sound pair 22)

10 Old town
/əʊ/ and /aʊ/

A

How to make the sound /əʊ/

 • /əʊ/ is a long sound. It moves from /ə/ to /ʊ/. Look at the diagram. Listen and say the sound. Target sound: /əʊ/

⚠ Note: When you say the sound /əʊ/ by itself, you say the letter O.

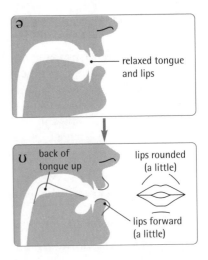

ə — relaxed tongue and lips

ʊ — back of tongue up / lips rounded (a little) / lips forward (a little)

B

Sound and spelling

 • /əʊ/ is spelled in different ways. Listen and repeat.

o	no	cold	post	close	drove	home	phone
ow	know	low	show	slow		
oa	boat					
oe	toe					

 • Listen and say these sentences.

1 I don't know.
2 My toes are cold.
3 She phoned me in October.
4 They showed us their home.

C

How to make the sound /aʊ/

 • /aʊ/ is a long sound. It moves from /a/ to /ʊ/. Look at the diagram. Listen and say the sound. Target sound: /aʊ/

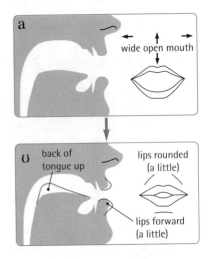

a — wide open mouth

ʊ — back of tongue up / lips rounded (a little) / lips forward (a little)

D

Sound and spelling

 • /aʊ/ is usually spelled **ow** or **ou**. Listen and repeat.

ow	how	now	vowel
ou	loud	mouth	sound

 • Listen and say these phrases.

1 a thousand pounds
2 loud vowel sounds
3 round the house
4 Countdown – three, two, one, now!

Exercises

10.1 Circle the word with a different vowel sound.

EXAMPLE

houses	(soup)	about	mountains
1 stone	gone	closed	coast
2 brown	flower	snow	town
3 old	over	lost	no
4 coach	boat	some	road

 Listen to check your answers. Check with the Key. Then listen and repeat.

10.2 Complete the text with some of the words from Exercise 10.1. All the missing words have /əʊ/ or /aʊ/.

It's an .... *old* .... *town* .... on the .... The .... are built with

.... You can get there by train, ... or .... In

winter there's a lot of .... and sometimes the .... the

.... is ....

 Listen to check your answers. Check with the Key. Then listen and repeat.

10.3 Listen and repeat these poems.

A67a **A pound**
I found a pound
down on the ground
and said, 'It's mine, I've got it.'
I looked around
and heard no sound
and put it in my pocket.

A67b **A letter**
A letter came
in the post
from the coast
– the one that I wanted the most.
It said, 'Don't be slow,
walk through the snow
and phone me when you are close.'

10.4 Listen and circle the word you hear. Check with the Key. If any of these are difficult for you, go to Section E3 *Sound pairs* for further practice.

A68 1 *coast / cost* (⇒ sound pair 11)
2 *boat / boot* (⇒ sound pair 6)
3 *woke / walk* (⇒ sound pair 12)

11 Pack your bags
/p/ and /b/

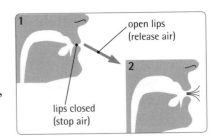

A How to make the sound /p/

 A69a
- Look at the diagrams. Listen and say the sound.
  1 Stop the air behind your lips.
  2 Open your lips to release the air. If you hold a piece of paper in front of your mouth when you open your lips, the paper moves. Target sound: /pə/

B Sound and spelling

 A69b
- /p/ is spelled **p** or **pp**. Listen and say these words:

  p   **p**en   **p**ush   sto**p**

  pp   ha**pp**y   sto**pp**ing

 A69c

Note: **p** is silent at the beginning of a few words. Listen and repeat. **p**sychology
Note: The word *cupboard* is pronounced /ˈkʌbəd/ – don't pronounce the **p**.
Note: **ph** is usually pronounced /f/: **ph**one, **ph**oto, autogra**ph**.
Note: /piː/ is the name of the letter P in the alphabet. People often say /piː/ for *pence*: 'It costs 75p.'

 A69d
- Listen and say these phrases.
  1 a **p**iece of **p**aper   2 **P**ush or **p**ull?   3 a dee**p** slee**p**   4 a chea**p** tri**p** round Euro**p**e

C How to make the sound /b/

A70a
- Look at the diagrams. Listen and say the sound.
  1 Stop the air behind your lips.
  2 Open your lips to release the air.

  /b/ is different from /p/ in two ways:
  1 If you hold a piece of paper in front of your mouth when you open your lips, the paper does not move.
  2 There is voicing (vibration from the throat). Target sound: /bə/

 A70b
- Listen and say the two sounds. /pə/ /bə/

D Sound and spelling

 A70c
- /b/ is spelled **b** or **bb**. Listen and say these words.
  big   **b**est   ro**b**   ro**bb**er   ver**b**

 A70d

Note: **b** is silent at the end of a few words. Listen and repeat. clim**b**   com**b**   thum**b**   bom**b**
Note: /biː/ is the name of the letter B in the alphabet.

 A70e
- Listen and say these phrases and sentences.

  1 **b**ig **b**usiness
  2 When was the **b**aby **b**orn?
  3 It's **b**etter to **b**ake your own **b**read than to **b**uy it.
  4 What's that **b**ig **b**uilding **b**etween the **b**ank and the li**b**rary?

 A70f
- Now listen and say these sentences with /p/ and /b/.

  1 Pamela's got a new job.
  2 Paul's got big problems with his neighbours.
  3 Can you remember Pete's phone number?
  4 Pack your bags and bring your passport.

 A70g

Important for listening

Sometimes you don't hear /p/ or /b/ clearly at the end of a word. Listen.

1 Stop!	Sto(p)!	3 Hey, Bob!	Hey, Bo(b)!
2 Don't drop that!	Don't dro(p) that!	4 the worldwide web	the worldwide we(b)

Exercises

11.1 Write the words. Choose from the words in the box.

back	beard	~~bill~~	black	bomb	book	boot	boots	bought	bread
build	but	butter	buy	pack	paper	part	party	pay	pepper	pie
piece	pool	pull	purse	put					

1 /bɪl/ ....bill.......
8 /pæk/ ....
15 /bæk/ ....

2 /piːs/ ....
9 /bɒm/ ....
16 /buːts/ ....

3 /baɪ/ ....
10 /ˈpepə/ ....
17 /puːl/ ....

4 /pɜːs/ ....
11 /ˈbʌtə/ ....
18 /brəd/ ....

5 /blæk/ ....
12 /paːt/ ....
19 /pʊt/ ....

6 /peɪ/ ....
13 /bʊk/ ....
20 /bɔːt/ ....

7 /bʌt/ ....
14 /ˈpaːti/ ....

A71 Listen to check your answers. Check with the Key. Then listen and repeat.

11.2 Complete the words with **p** or **b**.

1 Can you helᵨ me _aint the _edroom wardro_e?
2 Brian's _lond, and he's got a _ig _eard.
3 We're going to the _ub. It's my _rother's _irthday.
4 Where did I _ut my _lack _oots?
5 We asked the waiter to _ring the _ill, and it was
  dou_le what we expected!

A72 Listen to check your answers. Check with the Key.
Then listen and repeat.

Can you help me paint the
bedroom wardrobe?

11.3 Listen and fill the gaps.

A73 **EXAMPLE**
  Are you going to the ....shop....... ?
1 We'll have to change that ....
2 Looking for a .... ?
3 It isn't on the ....
4 Shall we give him a .... ?
5 Do we have to walk .... that hill?
6 .... the bus – I want to get off!
7 I .... you have a good time!
8 .... yourself!

Check with the Key. Then listen and repeat.

11.4 Listen and circle the word you hear. Check with the Key. If you find any of these difficult, go to
Section E3 *Sound pairs* for further practice.

A74 1 *pears / bears*   (⇒ sound pair 23)
2 *pear / fair*   (⇒ sound pair 24)
3 *copies / coffees*   (⇒ sound pair 24)

12 Twenty days
/t/ and /d/

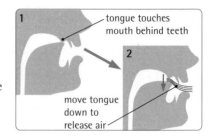

1 tongue touches mouth behind teeth
2
move tongue down to release air

How to make the sound /t/

 • Look at the diagrams. Listen and say the sound.
1 Stop the air with your tongue behind your teeth.
2 Move your tongue down to release the air. If you hold a piece of paper in front of your mouth when you move your tongue down, the paper moves. Target sound: /tə/

Sound and spelling

 • /t/ is usually spelled **t** or **tt**. Listen and say these words.

| t | tea | till | ten | top | two | twenty | water | bit | complete | eat | eight | light | suit |
| tt | better | bottle |

 • /t/ is sometimes spelled **ed** in past tenses. Listen and say these words.

ed   stopped   washed

 • /t/ is spelled **th** in a few names. Listen and say these words.

th   Thailand   Thames   Thomas

 Note: The letter **t** is silent in a few words. Listen and say these words. listen   castle

Note: /tiː/ is the name of the letter T in the alphabet. /tiː/ is also the word *tea*.

How to make the sound /d/

 • Look at the diagrams. Listen and say the sound.
1 Stop the air with your tongue behind your teeth.
2 Move your tongue down to release the air.

/d/ is different from /t/ in two ways:
1 If you hold a piece of paper in front of your mouth when you move your tongue down, the paper does not move.
2 There is voicing (vibration from the throat).
Target sound: /də/

1 tongue touches mouth behind teeth
2
move tongue down to release air

• Listen and say the two sounds. /tə/ /də/

Sound and spelling

 • /d/ is spelled **d** or **dd**. Listen and say these words.

| d | day | deep | do | door | did | food | good | head | ready |
| dd | add | address | ladder | middle |

Note: /diː/ is the name of the letter D in the alphabet.

 • Sometimes you don't hear the /t/ or /d/ clearly at the end of a word. Listen to the difference.

1 something to eat   something to ea(t)   3 the end of the road   the end of the roa(d)
2 turn on the light   turn on the ligh(t)   4 writing on the board   writing on the boar(d)

Important for listening

The vowel sound is longer before /d/ than before /t/. Listen.

roa(d)   wro(te)   boar(d)   bough(t)

• You often don't hear a /t/ or /d/ when it's between other consonant sounds, so *facts* sounds like *fax* and *next week* sounds like *necks week*. Listen.

A: Tell me all the fac(t)s.   B: I'll tell you nex(t) week.

Exercises

12.1 Listen and complete the sentences.

EXAMPLE What shall we do ....*next*.... week?

1 2001 was the .... time I went to Britain.
2 I .... some money in the street.
3 I worked hard .... week.
4 Do you know a .... place to eat near here?
5 I live in .... Road.
6 Is this the .... house?
7 Do you want some .... ?
8 Do you like my new .... ?

Check with the Key. Then listen again and repeat.

12.2 Listen and write the numbers of the words.

send ....   sent ....   wide ..*1*..   white ....
said ....   set ....   road ....   wrote ....

Check with the Key. Then listen again and repeat.

12.3 Listen and complete the sentences.

1 They .... us emails every day.
2 I .... all my money on CDs.
3 When it stopped snowing we went for a walk across the .... fields.
4 People .... houses next to the beach.

Check with the Key. Then listen again and repeat.

12.4 Listen and repeat these poems.

Too many twos
Tom and Tim were twins.
Tom said to Tim, 'Can I talk to you?'
Tim said to Tom, 'Ssh, wait a minute ...
One two is two
Two twos are four
Three twos are six
Four twos are eight
Five twos are ten ...'
Tom said to Tim, 'And what are two fives?'
Tim said to Tom, 'Two fives? Don't ask me!'

A difficult daughter
Doctor Dixon said to his daughter Daria,
'Don't go down town after dark – it's dangerous.'
Daria said, 'Don't worry, Dad, I won't. You know I never do.'
Next day when he came home for dinner, he said,
'Daria, dear, you didn't go down town after dark, did you?'
and she said, 'No, Dad, I didn't.'
But she did.
I don't know the details, but she definitely did.

12.5 Listen and circle the word you hear. Check with the Key. If you find any of these difficult, go to Section E3 *Sound pairs* for further practice.

1 *what / watch*   (⇒ sound pair 25)
2 *wide / white*   (⇒ sound pair 26)
3 *dry / try*   (⇒ sound pair 26)
4 *riding / writing*   (⇒ sound pair 26)
5 *taught / thought*   (⇒ sound pair 27)

13 Cats and dogs
/k/ and /g/

A How to make the sound /k/

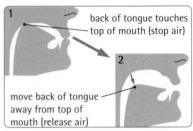

back of tongue touches top of mouth (stop air)

move back of tongue away from top of mouth (release air)

- Look at the diagrams. Listen and say the sound.
  1 Stop the air with the back of your tongue against the top of your mouth.
  2 Move your tongue to release the air. If you hold a piece of paper in front of your mouth when you release the air, the paper moves. Target sound: /kə/

B Sound and spelling

- /k/ is usually spelled **c**, **k** or **ck**, and sometimes **ch**. Listen and say these words.

c	car	cat	careful	clean	close	colour	fact
k	keep	key	kind	kitchen	desk	like	talk	walk
ck	back	black	check	pocket	tick		
ch	school	stomach	chemist	architect			

- /kw/ is often spelled **qu**. Listen and say these words. **qu**ick **qu**iet **qu**arter

- /ks/ is often spelled **x**. Listen and say these words. fa**x** si**x** ta**x**i

⚠ Note: The letter **k** is silent in a few words, e.g. *know, knee, knife.*

- Listen and say these sentences.
  1 Look in the kitchen cupboard. 2 Keep your keys in your pocket.

C How to make the sound /g/

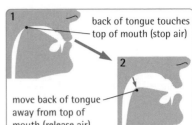

back of tongue touches top of mouth (stop air)

move back of tongue away from top of mouth (release air)

- Look at the diagrams. Listen and say the sound.
  1 Stop the air with the back of your tongue against the top of your mouth.
  2 Move your tongue to release the air.

  /g/ is different from /k/ in two ways:
  1 If you hold a piece of paper in front of your mouth when you release the air, the paper does not move.
  2 There is voicing (vibration from the throat). Target sound: /gə/

- Listen and say the two sounds. /kə/ /gə/

D Sound and spelling

- /g/ is usually spelled **g** or **gg**. Listen and say these words.
  garden **g**irl **g**lass **g**o **g**old a**g**o hun**g**ry ba**g** le**g** e**gg** bi**gg**er

- /gz/ is sometimes spelled **x**. Listen and say these words. e**x**am e**x**actly

⚠ Note: The letter **g** is silent in some words, e.g. *foreigner, sign, high, bought.*
Note: There is usually no /g/ sound in words like *sing, sings, singing, singer* (see Unit 19).
Note: Some words have a silent **u** after **g**. Listen and say these words. **gu**ess **gu**est dialo**gu**e

- Now listen and say these sentences.
  1 Can you guess the beginning of the dialogue? 2 Are you going jogging again?

You often don't hear /k/ or /g/ clearly in the middle or at the end of a word. Listen.

Important for listening

1 I li(k)ed the film – the a(c)ting was perfe(c)t. 3 It was a dar(k) night.
2 Do you li(ke) fo(lk) musi(c)? 4 What's your do(g) called?

Exercises

13.1 Write the words. Choose from the words in the box.

ache	again	ago	back	bag	big	bigger	bike	black	called	cake
carry	classical	coffee	cold	comb	come	copy	gave	get	~~give~~	great
grey	guess	guest	keys	kiss	walk	work				

1 /gɪv/ ......give......   8 /eɪk/ ....   15 /bæg/ ....
2 /bɪg/ ....   9 /gest/ ....   16 /'bɪgə/ ....
3 /get/ ....   10 /bæk/ ....   17 /kəʊld/ ....
4 /kəʊm/ ....   11 /'kɒfi/ ....   18 /'kæri/ ....
5 /kiːz/ ....   12 /ə'gen/ ....   19 /wɜːk/ ....
6 /keɪk/ ....   13 /wɔːk/ ....   20 /greɪ/ ....
7 /kɪs/ ....   14 /kɔːld/ ....

(B4) Listen to check your answers. Check with the Key. Then listen and repeat.

13.2 Complete the words. They all have /k/ or /g/ sounds.

1 Can I <u>c</u>arry your ba_s?
2 Give me a bi_ _iss.
3 You _ave me _old _offee a_ain.
4 A _rey _at with _reen eyes wal_ed into the
 _arden.
5 The _uests would li_e e_ _s for brea_fast.

(B5) Listen to check your answers.
Check with the Key. Then listen and repeat.

Can I carry your bags?

13.3 Listen and fill the gaps.

(B6) **EXAMPLE**
 It's time to go ......back...... .
1 Shall we .... ?
2 I came by ....
3 When you go out, ... the
 ....
4 I'm going to buy a new .... tomorrow.
5 A: You don't .... in your tea, do you?
 B: I do, in ....
6 It's only seven o'clock and it's already ....
7 Listen and ....
8 Mark your answer with a ....

Listen to check your answers. Check with the Key. Then listen and repeat.

13.4 Listen and circle the word you hear. Check with the Key. If you find any of these difficult, go to
 Section E3 *Sound pairs* for further practice.

(B7) 1 *back / bag* (⇒ sound pair 28)
 2 *cold / gold* (⇒ sound pair 28)

14 November the first
/f/ and /v/

A How to make the sound /f/

 • Look at the diagram. Listen and say the sound. There is no voicing (vibration from the throat), and you can feel the air on your hand in front of your mouth. Target sound: /fffff/

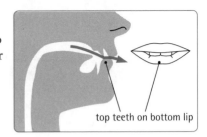

top teeth on bottom lip

B Sound and spelling

 • /f/ is usually spelled f or ff, and sometimes ph or gh. Listen and say these words.

f	feel	first	café	after	leaf
ff	off	coffee			
ph	phone	autograph			
gh	laugh				

 • Listen and say these phrases and sentences.

1 forty-five
2 a family photo
3 I'm feeling fine.
4 the fourteenth of February
5 When I asked for her autograph she just laughed.

C How to make the sound /v/

 • Look at the diagram. Listen and say the sound. There is voicing (vibration from the throat), and you can feel less air on your hand in front of your mouth then when you say /f/. Target sound: /vvvvv/

 • Listen and say the two sounds.

/fffff/ /vvvvv/

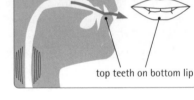

top teeth on bottom lip

D Sound and spelling

 • /v/ is usually spelled v. Listen and say these words.

very travel every have leave

⚠ Note: In the name *Stephen*, ph is pronounced /v/.

 • Listen and say these phrases and sentences.

1 We're leaving at five past seven.
2 a visa for a seven-day visit
3 Stephen lives in a village.

Exercises

14.1   Write these words.

EXAMPLE
/fəʊn/ .... *phone* ....
1 /faɪv/ ....
2 /ˈvɪzɪt/ ....
3 /fɜːst/ ....
4 /friː/ ....
5 /liːv/ ....
6 /ˈfəʊtəʊ/ ....

B10   Listen to check your answers. Check with the Key. Then listen and repeat.

14.2   Complete the titles of the pictures using these words.

| few | voices | fast | seventh | ~~fine~~ | forks | vegetables | lift | five | floor | view |
| driving | knives | | | | | | | | | |

1 A ..... *fine* ....

4 ....

2 .... too ....

5 A ....

3 .... and ....

6 The .... to the ....

B11   Listen to check your answers. Check with the Key. Then listen and repeat.

14.3   Listen and repeat these poems.

B12a   **November the first**
November the first
Five leaves left
One leaf falls
Four leaves left.

B12b   **The traveller**
'A visitor? Having fun?
A fine day for travelling,'
he said.
'A café? A phone? Here?
I'm afraid not,'
he laughed.
'You'll find one in the village.
Far? No, not very far.
The ferry over the river.
Then a few more miles –
five, or seven, or eleven ...'

14.4   Listen and circle the word you hear. Check with the Key. If you find any of these difficult, go to Section E3 *Sound pairs* for further practice.

B13   1 *few / view*   (⇒ sound pair 29)
2 *leaf / leave*   (⇒ sound pair 29)
3 *copy / coffee*   (⇒ sound pair 24)

15 Both together
/θ/ and /ð/

How to make the sound /θ/

 • Look at the diagram. Listen and say the sound. Make loose contact between the tongue and the back of the teeth and push the air through the gap. There is no voicing (vibration from the throat). Target sound: /θθθθθ/

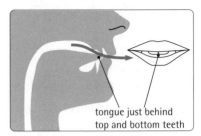

tongue just behind top and bottom teeth

B

Sound and spelling

 • /θ/ is spelled **th**. Listen and say these words.

thin **th**anks **th**irty **th**eatre **th**umb **Th**ursday **th**irsty **th**ree
bo**th** mon**th** mou**th** nor**th** sou**th**
bir**th**day

 • Listen and say these sentences.

1 I **th**ought April the twelf**th** was a Tuesday, but it's a **Th**ursday.
2 A: I've got **th**ree bir**th**days this mon**th**.
   B: **Th**ree bir**th**days? What do you mean?
   A: My wife's, my son's and my daughter's!
3 It's **th**irteen degrees in the nor**th**, and **th**irty in the sou**th**.
4 A: One **th**ird is **th**irty-**th**ree per cent, isn't it?
   B: **Th**irty-**th**ree and a **th**ird per cent, to be exact.

C

How to make the sound /ð/

 • Look at the diagram. Listen and say the sound. Make loose contact between the tongue and the back of the teeth and push the air through the gap. /ð/ is different from /θ/ because there is voicing (vibration from the throat). Target sound: /ðððð/

tongue just behind top and bottom teeth

 • Listen and say the two sounds.
/θθθθθ/ /ðððð/

D

Sound and spelling

 • /ð/ is spelled **th**. Listen and say these words.

this **th**at **th**ese **th**ose **th**en **th**ey fa**th**er mo**th**er bro**th**er o**th**er toge**th**er
wea**th**er wi**th**out brea**th**e wi**th**

 • Listen and say these sentences.

1 A: Can I have one of **th**ose, please?
   B: **Th**ese?
   A: No, the o**th**ers, over **th**ere.
2 A: Two coffees, please.
   B: Wi**th** milk?
   A: One wi**th**, and one wi**th**out.

⚠ Note: th is usually pronounced /θ/ or /ð/, but sometimes /t/: Thailand Thames Thomas

Exercises

15.1   Write these words.

EXAMPLE
/ðæt/ ....that........

1 /mʌnθ/ ....
2 /ðen/ ....
3 /θɪn/ ....
4 /ðeɪ/ ....
5 /wɪð/ ....
6 /'bɜːθdeɪ/ ....

(B16)   Listen to check your answers. Check with the Key. Then listen and repeat.

15.2   Listen. Which words have /θ/, and which words have /ð/?

(B17)
1 What are you <u>thinking</u> about?
2 Can I have <u>another</u>?
3 Are you good at <u>maths</u>?
4 Where's <u>the</u> <u>bathroom</u>?
5 What are <u>those</u> <u>things</u> over <u>there</u>?
6 Is the plural of '<u>tooth</u>' '<u>teeth</u>'?
7 Is today the <u>fourth</u> or the <u>fifth</u>?

words with /θ/	words with /ð/
....thinking....	....
....	....
....	....
....	....
....	
....	
....	

Listen to check your answers. Check with the Key. Then listen and repeat.

15.3   Listen and complete the sentences.

(B18)
1 The ....weather.... will be fine for .... next ....
days. .... , on .... , ... 'll be some rain in the ....
The .... will be dry and sunny, but only about .... degrees.
2 A: I'm thinking of going to the .... tonight.
   B: Me too! Let's .... go
   .... !
3 A: Are you .... ?
   B: No, ...
4 A: .... are my .... and
   .... , about ....
   years ago. And .... is my older
   .... – he was about
   .... years old.
   B: And .... baby – is
   .... you?
   A: Yes, ... 's me, ...
   my .... in my .... !

Check with the Key. Then listen again and repeat.

4

15.4   Listen and circle the word you hear. Check with the Key. If you find any of these difficult, go to Section E3 *Sound pairs* for further practice.

(B19)
1 *thing / sing*   (⇒ sound pair 30)
2 *three / tree*   (⇒ sound pair 27)

16 It's the wrong size, isn't it?
/s/ and /z/

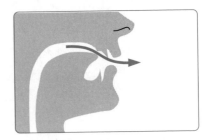

A | How to make the sound /s/

- Look at the diagram. Listen and say the sound. There is some contact between the tongue and the teeth at the sides of the mouth. There is no voicing (vibration from the throat). Target sound: /sssss/

B | Sound and spelling

- /s/ is usually spelled **s**, **ss** or **c**, and sometimes **sc**. Listen and say these words.

s	**s**it **s**i**s**ter bu**s**
ss	cla**ss** gla**ss**es
c	**c**ity **c**ircle pen**c**il pla**c**e poli**c**e pronoun**c**e
sc	**sc**ience **sc**issors

- The letter **x** is usually pronounced /ks/. Listen and say these words.

  si**x**   ne**x**t

- Listen and say these phrases and sentences.

  1 **s**ummer in the **c**ity
  2 Have you **s**een my gla**ss**es?
  3 **S**o, I'll **s**ee you in the **s**ame pla**c**e ne**x**t **S**aturday.
  4 I **s**aw your **s**i**s**ter on the bu**s** yesterday.
  5 My **sc**ience le**ss**ons were the mo**s**t intere**s**ting.

C | How to make the sound /z/

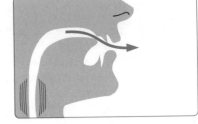

- Look at the diagram. Listen and say the sound. There is some contact between the tongue and the teeth at the sides of the mouth. /z/ is different from /s/ because there is voicing (vibration from the throat). Target sound: /zzzzz/

- Listen and say the two sounds.

  /sssss/ /zzzzz/

D | Sound and spelling

- /z/ is usually spelled **s** or **z**, and sometimes **ss** or **zz**. Listen and say these words.

s	give**s** **s**i**s**ter**s** ea**s**y hu**s**band ro**s**e**s**
z	**z**oo **z**ero si**z**e
ss	sci**ss**ors
zz	ja**zz**

- Listen and say these sentences.

  1 What time does the **z**oo close?
  2 A: My favourite music is ja**zz**.
     B: Really? Well, it's alway**s** interesting, but it isn't alway**s** ea**s**y to listen to.
  3 Ro**s**e**s** are my favourite flowers.

Exercises

16.1 Write these words.

EXAMPLE /saɪz/ ....size........
1 /seɪ/ ....
2 /sæt/ ....
3 /liːvz/ ....
4 /iːst/ ....
5 /taɪmz/ ....
6 /ˈɡlɑːsɪz/ ....

(B22) Listen to check your answers. Check with the Key. Then listen and repeat.

16.2 1 Which two days of the week have /s/? ....
2 Which three days of the week have /z/? ....
3 Which three months of the year have /s/? ....August........ ....

(B23) Listen to check your answers. Check with the Key. Then listen and repeat.

16.3 Listen and write the /s/ and /z/ sounds in each word.

(B24) EXAMPLES sit /s/   easy /z/   places /s/ /z/
1 these / /
2 size / / / /
3 style / /
4 please / /
5 isn't / /
6 pronounce / /
7 dress / /
8 it's / /
9 certainly / /
10 words / /
11 suits / / / /

Listen to check your answers. Check with the Key. Then listen and repeat.

16.4 Fill the gaps with the words from Exercise 16.3.

1 A: Do you like this ....dress........? B: The .... you, but
.... the wrong ...., ... it?
2 A: Can you .... for me, ...?
B: Yes, ...

(B25) Listen to check your answers. Check with the Key. Then listen and repeat.

16.5 Listen and repeat this poem.

(B26) **One day**

Mondays to Fridays –
Gets up.
Walks to the station.
Waits for the train.
Gets off at the fourth stop.
Walks to the office.
Sits in the office.
Has lunch.
Sits in the office
Walks to the station.
Comes home.
Thinks: 'One day ...'

Saturdays and Sundays –
Gets up. Late.
Does the washing.
Goes shopping.
Comes home.
Watches TV.
Goes out.
Eats out.
Comes home.
Watches TV.
Thinks: 'One day ...'

One day –
Gets up. Early.
Goes to the station.
Waits for the train.
Doesn't get off at the fourth stop.
Doesn't get off at the fifth stop.
Stays on the train.
Where does it go?
Watches through the windows.

16.6 Listen and circle the word you hear. Check with the Key. If you find any of these difficult, go to Section E3 *Sound pairs* for further practice.

(B27) 1 *place* / *plays* (⇒ sound pair 31)
2 *zoo* / *Sue* (⇒ Sound pair 31)
3 *so* / *show* (⇒ sound pair 32)
4 *sing* / *thing* (⇒ sound pair 30)

17 Fresh fish, usually
/ʃ/ and /ʒ/

How to make the sound /ʃ/

 B28a • Look at the diagram. Listen and say the sound. Your tongue points upwards towards the roof of your mouth. There is some contact between the tongue and the teeth at the sides of the mouth. There is no voicing (vibration from the throat). Target sound: /ʃʃʃʃʃ/

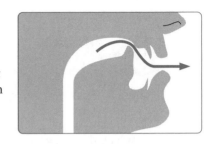

Sound and spelling

 B28b • /ʃ/ is usually spelled **sh**. Listen and say these words.

shop   fa**sh**ion   ca**sh**   fre**sh**   wa**sh**   mu**sh**room

 B28c • But /ʃ/ is sometimes spelled in different ways. Listen and say these words.

c	o**c**ean
ch	ma**ch**ine
ci	deli**ci**ous spe**ci**al
s	**s**ugar **s**ure
ss	Ru**ss**ia
ti	interna**ti**onal

B28d • Listen and say these sentences.

1 This is a very spe**ci**al pronuncia**ti**on ma**ch**ine.
2 All our food is fre**sh**, and we serve deli**ci**ous interna**ti**onal spe**ci**alities.
3 A: You didn't put **s**ugar in my tea, did you?
   B: No.
   A: Are you **s**ure?

This is a very special pronunciation machine.

How to make the sound /ʒ/

 B29a • Look at the diagram. Listen and say the sound. Your tongue points upwards towards the roof of your mouth. There is some contact between the tongue and the teeth at the sides of the mouth. /ʒ/ is different from /ʃ/ because there is voicing (vibration from the throat). Target sound: /ʒʒʒʒʒ/

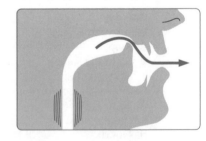

B29b • Listen and say the two sounds.

/ʃʃʃʃʃ/ /ʒʒʒʒʒ/

Sound and spelling

 B29c • There are not many words with /ʒ/. It is usually spelled **si** or **s**. Listen and say these words.

televi**si**on   A**s**ia   u**s**ually

 B29d • Listen and say these sentences.

A: Do you like sport?
B: Yes … but only on televi**si**on, u**s**ually!

Exercises

17.1 Write these words.

EXAMPLE
/ˈʃʊgə/ ....*sugar*....
1 /fɪʃ/ ....
2 /ˈsteɪʃn/ ....
3 /ˈfɪnɪʃ/ ....
4 /ʃaʊt/ ....
5 /ʃɔːt/ ....
6 /dɪʃ/ ....

🎧 B30 Listen to check your answers. Check with the Key. Then listen and repeat.

17.2 Listen and complete the text.
🎧 B31

> # Recipe
>
> Take your ....*cash*.... .
> Go to the ....
> Buy some ....
> and some ....
> Take them home.
> .... them.
> Cook them for a .... time.
> Put them in a ....
> Eat them.
> .... , '.................................... !'

Check with the Key. Then listen and repeat.

17.3 Listen and complete the sentences.
🎧 B32

1 Yes, we're an .... business.
   We're based in .... , but we fly
   to anywhere in .... and the
   Pacific ....
2 A: Why are you .... at that
      .... ?
   B: It's eaten my .... !

Check with the Key. Then listen and repeat.

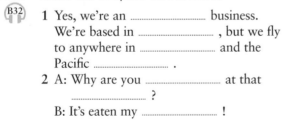

17.4 Listen and circle the word you hear. Check
with the Key. If you find any of these
difficult, go to Section E3 *Sound pairs* for
further practice.

🎧 B33 1 *shoe / Sue* (⇒ sound pair 32)
        2 *shoes / choose* (⇒ sound pair 33)

18 Chips and juice
/tʃ/ and /dʒ/

A   How to make the sound /tʃ/

 B34a
- Look at the diagram. Listen and say the sound. There is no voicing (vibration from the throat). /tʃ/ is like /t/ + /ʃ/ together. Target sound: /tʃə/

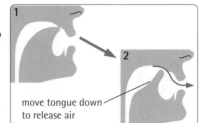

move tongue down to release air

B   Sound and spelling

 B34b
- /tʃ/ is usually spelled **ch**, **t**, or **tch**. Listen and say these words.

ch	**ch**ips	**ch**oose	Mar**ch**	whi**ch**
t	future	question	
tch	ca**tch**	wa**tch**	ki**tch**en

⚠ **Note:** The name of the letter H is /eɪtʃ/. Listen and repeat.

B34c
B34d   **Note:** In the word *Czech*, cz is pronounced /tʃ/, and ch is pronounced /k/. The words *check*, *cheque* and *Czech* all sound the same: /tʃek/. Listen and repeat. (See Section E8 *Homophones*.)

 B34e
- Listen and say these sentences.
  1 Whi**ch** questions did you **ch**oose in the exam?
  2 The pi**ct**ure in the ki**tch**en is by a **Cz**ech artist.

C   How to make the sound /dʒ/

 B35a
- Look at the diagram. Listen and say the sound. There is voicing (vibration from the throat). /dʒ/ is like /d/ + /ʒ/ together. Target sound: /dʒə/

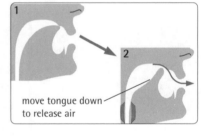

move tongue down to release air

B35b
- Listen and say the two sounds.

  /tʃə/ /dʒə/

D   Sound and spelling

 B35c
- /dʒ/ is usually spelled **j**, **g**, **ge** or **dge**. Listen and say these words.

j	**j**am	**j**acket	**j**eans	**j**ob	**j**et
g	**g**eneral				
ge	a**ge**	lar**ge**			
dge	fri**dge**				

⚠ **Note:** The name of the letter G is /dʒiː/, and the name of the letter J is /dʒeɪ/. Listen and repeat.

 B35e
- Listen and say these sentences.
  1 Who's that wearing a lar**ge** oran**ge j**acket?
  2 There's some **j**uice in the fri**dge**.
  3 Langua**ge**s are a bri**dge** between people.

Exercises

18.1 Write these words.

EXAMPLE /dʒæm/ ....*jam*...........
1 /wɒtʃ/ ....   4 /lɑːdʒ/ ....   7 /tʃeə/ ....
2 /dʒɒb/ ....   5 /dʒuːs/ ....   8 /eɪdʒ/ ....
3 /tʃɪps/ ....   6 /dʒæz/ ....

(B36) Listen to check your answers. Check with the Key. Then listen and repeat.

18.2 Listen and circle the odd one out.

(B37) EXAMPLE
    larger   generally   (guess)   fri<u>dg</u>e
1 village   get   <u>G</u>ermany   page
2 coa<u>ch</u>   <u>ch</u>eck   <u>Ch</u>ristmas   tempera<u>t</u>ure
3 <u>J</u>une   vegetable   give   cabbage
4 sta<u>ti</u>on   Ru<u>ss</u>ian   pic<u>t</u>ure   informa<u>ti</u>on

Listen to check your answers. Check with the Key. Then listen and repeat.

18.3 Listen and repeat these sentences.

(B38) 1 I went to a small Russian village.   4 Look at this page of information.
    2 Cabbage is my favourite vegetable.   5 I'm going to the coach station.
    3 I was in Germany at Christmas.   6 Can you check the temperature, please?

18.4 Listen and put these words into two groups.

(B39)

~~teacher~~	lounge	bridge	chair	large	chicken	cheap	juice	Dutch
language	chips	orange	cheese	dangerous				

words with /tʃ/   **words with /dʒ/**
.....*teacher*.....   ....
....
....
....

Listen to check your answers. Check with the Key. Then listen and repeat.

18.5 Fill the gaps with words from Exercise 18.4.

1 Something to drink: ......*orange*...... ....
2 Something to eat, from a European country: ....
3 A ....
4 Someone who teaches English or Chinese: a ....
5 A hot meal: .... and ....
6 A ....
7 A big room to sit and relax in: a ....

(B40) Listen to check your answers. Check with the Key. Then listen and repeat.

3

18.6 Listen and circle the word you hear. Check with the Key. If you find any of these difficult, go to Section E3 *Sound pairs* for further practice.

(B41) 1 *watch / wash*   (⇒ sound pair 33)
    2 *shoes / choose*   (⇒ sound pair 33)
    3 *what's / watch*   (⇒ sound pair 25)
    4 *coach / coats*   (⇒ sound pair 25)

6

19 My hungry uncle
/m/, /n/ and /ŋ/

A

How to make the sound /m/

 • When you say /m/, the air comes through your nose, not your mouth. Look at the diagram. Listen and say the sound. Your lips are together, and there is voicing. Target sound: /mmmmm/

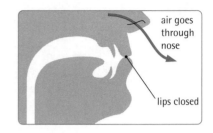

air goes through nose

lips closed

B

Sound and spelling

 • /m/ is usually spelled **m** or **mm**, but sometimes **mb** or **mn**. Listen and say these words.

m		me	more	lemon	swim	film	some	sometimes
mm	summer		**mb**	comb		**mn**	autumn	

 • Listen and say these phrases.
1 sometimes in summer   2 more for you, most for me   3 in the middle of the film

C

How to make the sound /n/

 • When you say /n/, the air comes through your nose, not your mouth. Look at the diagram. Listen and say the sound. Your tongue is pressed against the roof of your mouth behind the teeth, and there is voicing. Target sound: /nnnnn/

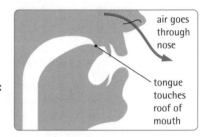

air goes through nose

tongue touches roof of mouth

D

Sound and spelling

 • /n/ is usually spelled **n**, but sometimes **nn** or **kn**. Listen and say these words.

n	new	now	sun	one	gone
nn	dinner	sunny			
kn	knew	know	knife		

 • Listen and say these phrases.
1 a sunny afternoon   2 sun and moon   3 nine months

E

How to make the sound /ŋ/

 • When you say /ŋ/, the air comes through your nose, not your mouth. Look at the diagram. Listen and say the sound. The back of your tongue is pressed against the roof of your mouth, and there is voicing. Target sound: /ŋŋŋŋŋ/

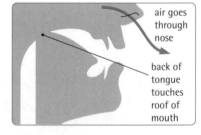

air goes through nose

back of tongue touches roof of mouth

 • Listen and say the three sounds. /mmmm/ /nnnnn/ /ŋŋŋŋŋ/

F

Sound and spelling

• /ŋ/ is usually spelled **ng**.
The letter **n** is pronounced /ŋ/ if there is a /k/ or /g/ after it.
ng is sometimes /ŋ/ (e.g. **singer**) and sometimes /ŋg/ (e.g. **finger**).
nk is always pronounced /ŋk/.

 • Listen and say these words.

/ŋ/	evening	long	sing	singer	thing
/ŋk/	bank	thanks	think	uncle	
/ŋg/	angry	finger	hungry	longer	single

 • Listen and say these phrases.
1 thinking about things 2 a long evening singing songs 3 a hungry man is an angry man

Exercises

19.1   Write these words.

EXAMPLE
/mɔː/ .... more ....
1 /muːn/ ....
2 /rɒŋ/ ....
3 /drɪŋk/ ....
4 /ˈʌŋkl/ ....

5 /naɪvz/ ....
6 /kəʊm/ ....
7 /θɪŋ/ ....
8 /ˈstrɒŋgə/ ....

(B45)   Listen to check your answers. Check with the Key. Then listen and repeat.

19.2   Write the words. Two are with /n/ and three with /ŋ/.

words with /n/   **words with /ŋ/**
.... knee ....

....

                 ....

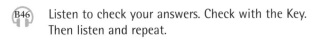

(B46)   Listen to check your answers. Check with the Key.
Then listen and repeat.

19.3   Complete the titles of the pictures using these words.

room   nine   wrong   single   ~~warm~~   uncle   languages   evening   hungry   answer

1 A .... warm ....   2 A ....   3 My ....   4 A ....   5 ....

....

(B47)   Listen to check your answers. Check with the Key. Then listen and repeat.

19.4   Look at the picture and complete the sentences.

1 The woman's .... listening .... to the radio and ....
2 The phone's ....
3 The cat's ....
4 It's ....

(B48)   Listen to check your answers. Check with the Key. Then listen and
repeat.

19.5

Listen and circle the word you hear. Check with the Key.
If you find any of these difficult, go to Section E3
Sound pairs for further practice.

(B49)   1 *ran / rang*   (⇒ sound pair 34)
2 *thing / think*   (⇒ sound pair 34)
3 *might / night*   (⇒ sound pair 35)
4 *some / sung*   (⇒ sound pair 35)
5 *some / sun*   (⇒ sound pair 35)

20 How many hours? /h/

A How to make the sound /h/

 • Look at the diagram. Listen and say the sound. The air comes through a small gap at the back of the mouth. There is no voicing. Target sound: /hə/

B Sound and spelling

 • /h/ is usually spelled **h**, but it is spelled **wh** in a few words. Listen and say these words.

h	**h**at	**h**ere	**h**elp	**h**ot	**h**ow	be**h**ind
wh	**wh**o	**wh**ose	**wh**ole			

 • A few words begin with a silent letter **h**. Listen and say these words.

hour   honest

 • Listen and say these sentences.

> Hi, hello, how are you?

1 **H**i, **h**ello, **h**ow are you?
2 **Wh**ose **h**at is this?
3 It's **h**ot in **h**ere.
4 We **h**ad a **wh**ole month's **h**oliday.
5 Can you **h**elp me for **h**alf an hour?
6 **Wh**o's **wh**o?

Important for listening

Sometimes you don't hear an /h/ sound at the beginning of *he, him, her, hers, his, had, have, has.* (See Units 37–40.) Listen.

1 Is he there?
2 Have you seen him?
3 Has he got time?
4 Do you know her?
5 He went to visit his family.

Exercises

20.1 Write these words.

EXAMPLE
/hed/ .... *head* ....
1 /hæt/ ....
2 /haʊ/ ....
3 /həʊm/ ....
4 /hɑːf/ ....
5 /haɪ/ ....
6 /huː/ ....

(B51) Listen to check your answers. Check with the Key. Then listen and repeat.

20.2 Listen and complete the dialogue.
(B52)
A: Excuse me, can you tell me ....*how*........ to get to the castle?
B: Yes. Go past the .... and the .... , then there's a road ....
   those .... You go up a .... , and the castle's at the top.
A: Thanks for your .... !

Check with the Key. Then listen and repeat.

20.3 Complete the titles of the pictures using these words.

half	hand	home	perhaps	who	happy	happen	hours	~~helping~~	how
hi	house	holiday	how	history					

1 A ....*helping*....
....

2 A ....
....

3 .... many
.... ?

4 ....
.... ?

5 .... a
....

6 .... did it
.... ?

7 .... !
.... 's at
.... ?

(B53) Listen to check your answers. Check with the Key. Then listen and repeat.

20.4 Listen and circle the word you hear. Check with the Key. If you find any of these difficult, go to
Section E3 *Sound pairs* for further practice.

(B54)
1 *hear* / *ear*   (⇒ sound pair 37)
2 *high* / *eye*   (⇒ sound pair 37)

21 That's life!
/l/

A — How to make the sound /l/

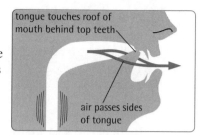

tongue touches roof of mouth behind top teeth

air passes sides of tongue

B55a • Look at the diagram. Listen and say the sound. The tip of your tongue touches the roof of your mouth just behind the top teeth, the air passes the sides of the tongue, and there is voicing. (If you prepare to say /l/ but breathe in instead of out, you feel cold air on the sides of your tongue.) Target sound: /lllll/

B — Sound and spelling

B55b • /l/ is spelled l or ll. Listen and say these words.

| l | learn | leave | language | lovely | alone | feel | help | English |
| ll | tall | well | yellow | | | | | |

B55c • /l/ is long at the end of some words. Listen and say these words.

peop**l**e   simp**l**e   unc**l**e   litt**l**e

B55d • In some words, the letter l is silent. Listen and say these words.

half   talk   could

B55e • Listen and say these sentences.

1 When sha**ll** we leave?
2 Are you alone?
3 How do you feel?
4 Can I he**l**p you?
5 Look at those lovely little yellow flowers.
6 Learning a language can be difficult for some people.

Exercises

21.1 Write these words.

EXAMPLE
/fiːl/ ...... feel ......
1 /leɪt/ ....
2 /laɪt/ ....
3 /lɑːdʒ/ ....
4 /kəʊld/ ....
5 /ˈteɪbl/ ....
6 /ˈæpl/ ....
7 /ˈlɜːnɪŋ/ ....
8 /bɪˈləʊ/ ....

B56 Listen to check your answers. Check with the Key. Then listen and repeat.

21.2 Look at the pictures and complete the sentences using these words.

> hello   double   middle   bottle   ~~letter~~   litter   table   alphabet   single   letter
> little   apple

1 Did you say the ...... letter ...... box or the .... bin?
2 .... My name's L. I'm the twelfth .... of the ....
3 There's an .... in the .... of the ....
4 Would you like a .... room or a .... ?
5 What's in that .... ?

B57 Listen to check your answers. Check with the Key. Then listen and repeat.

21.3 Listen and complete the story.
B58

Monday	My bus was ...... late ....
Tuesday	I .... my wallet.
Wednesday	I .... off a ladder.
Thursday	I caught a ....
Friday	I .... at work.
That's	.... !

Check with the Key. Then listen and repeat.

21.4 Listen and circle the word you hear. Check with the Key. If you find any of these difficult, go to
Section E3 *Sound pairs* for further practice.

B59 1 *light / right*   (⇒ sound pair 36)
2 *collect / correct*   (⇒ sound pair 36)

22 What terrible weather!
/r/

A How to make the sound /r/

 • Look at the diagram. Listen and say the sound. The tip of your tongue points backwards towards the roof of the mouth, there is some contact between the tongue and the teeth at the sides of the mouth, and there is voicing. Target sound: /rrrrr/

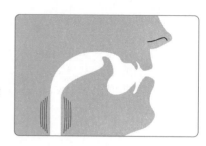

B Sound and spelling

 • /r/ is usually spelled **r** or **rr**, and sometimes **wr**. Listen and say these words.

r	red	ready	really	right	road	room
rr	ferry	sorry				
wr	**wr**ap	**wr**ist	**wr**ite	**wr**itten	**wr**ote	

 • Listen and say these phrases and sentences.

1 What are you **r**eading?
2 I'm **r**eally so**rr**y – your **r**oom isn't **r**eady.
3 I don't know if I'm **r**ight or **wr**ong.
4 Too much **wr**iting makes my **wr**ist ache.
5 t**r**avelling by fe**rr**y
6 **wr**apping p**r**esents for Christmas

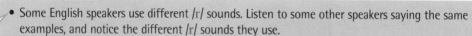

Important for listening

• Some English speakers use different /r/ sounds. Listen to some other speakers saying the same examples, and notice the different /r/ sounds they use.

 • Where there's a letter **r** in a word, most people in England, Wales and Australia only pronounce it if there's a vowel sound after it, in the same word or the next word. Listen.

four	no /r/
forty	no /r/
four days	no /r/
four eggs	/r/ is pronounced
four hours	/r/ is pronounced

• But most people in America, Scotland, Ireland and the south-west of England always pronounce /r/ where there's a letter **r** in the spelling. Listen.

four	/r/ is pronounced
forty	/r/ is pronounced
four days	/r/ is pronounced
four eggs	/r/ is pronounced
four hours	/r/ is pronounced

 ⚠ Note: The name of the letter R in the alphabet is /ɑː/ – or /ɑːr/ for those speakers who always pronounce the letter r. Listen.

Exercises

22.1 Put these words in the correct places, in their normal spelling.

/ruːm/ /ˈɪərɪŋ/ /ɔːlˈredi/ /ˈrekɔːdz/ /reɪn/ /əˈraɪv/ /raʊnd/ /ˈbɒrəʊd/ /əˈdres/
/ˈrʌnɪŋ/ /ˈrʌbɪʃ/ /ˈhʌri/ /r̶ɒk̶/ /ˈterɪbl/ /ˈrɪəli/ /reɪs/ /raɪt/ /ˈwʌri/ /ˈredi/ /əˈfreɪd/

1 Hey, look! I found these old ......*rock*...... .... in a .... bin!
2 .... again – what .... weather!
3 Are you .... sure this is the .... ?
4 Stop .... the .... ! We've got to get .... to
 go out.
5 A: Oh, no, I've lost an ....
 B: I'm .... Anna .... it!
6 A: .... up!
 B: Why? It isn't a ....
 A: We're .... late!
 B: Don't .... , they'll wait till we ....

🎧 B61 Listen to check your answers. Check with the Key. Then listen and repeat.

22.2 Look at the words with **r** in the spelling. Listen and put a tick (✓) by them if the **r** is pronounced, and
🎧 B62 a cross (✗) if the **r** is not pronounced.

1 A: Where ✓ did you park the car?
 B: I'm not sure. I think it was just around the corner.
2 A: Have you ever heard of square oranges?
 B: No, never!
3 A: Can you play the guitar?
 B: I can play the guitar and sing.
4 A: Are we far away from the road?
 B: Well, it's rather hard to say …

Check with the Key. Then listen and repeat.

22.3 Listen and circle the word you hear. Check with the Key. If you find any of these difficult, go to
Section E3 *Sound pairs* for further practice.

🎧 B63
1 *light / right* (⇒ sound pair 36)
2 *long / wrong* (⇒ sound pair 36)
3 *collect / correct* (⇒ sound pair 36)

23 What's the news?
/w/ and /j/

A How to make the sound /w/

 • Look at the diagram. Listen and say the sound. /w/ is like a very short /uː/ sound. Target sound: /wə/

lips round

lips forward

B Sound and spelling

 • The sound /w/ is usually spelled **w**, and sometimes **wh**, and there are some words with other spellings of /w/. Listen and say these words.

w	week	wet	way	warm	well	weather	windy	away	always	twelve		swim
wh	what	white	which	where								
	one	language	question	quiet	square							

⚠ **Note: qu** is often pronounced /kw/.

 Note: /w/ is not pronounced in some words. Listen and repeat.

answer   two   who   whole   write   wrong

 • Listen and say these phrases and sentences.

1 swimming in warm water
2 twenty-one words
3 What's the answer?
4 quarter to twelve on Wednesday
5 twenty-two languages

6 the wrong word
7 the whole world
8 question and answer
9 Where will you be waiting?

C How to make the sound /j/

 • Look at the diagram. Listen and say the sound. /j/ is like a very short /iː/ sound. Target sound: /jə/

small gap at top of mouth

D Sound and spelling

 • The sound /j/ is usually spelled **y**, but has different spellings in some words.

/juː/ is often spelled **u** or **ew**. Listen and say these words.

y	yes	yesterday	year	young				
/juː/	usual	student	university	new	view	interview	beautiful	queue
	Europe /ˈjʊərəp/							

 • Listen and say these phrases and sentences.

1 a young university student
2 a beautiful view
3 waiting in a queue for an interview
4 the European Union
5 I usually walk to work but I used the car yesterday.

 • American speakers don't pronounce /j/ in some words like *new* and *student*. Listen.

Important for listening

with /j/: Are you a new student? /njuː ˈstjuːdənt/

without /j/: Are you a new student? /nuː ˈstuːdənt/

Exercises

23.1 Write these words.

EXAMPLE

/ˈjʌŋgə/ ....*younger*....

1 /njuːz/ ....
2 /fjuː/ ....
3 /jet/ ....
4 /ˈwiːkend/ ....
5 /tjuːnz/ ....

6 /wen/ ....
7 /ˈmjuːzɪk/ ....
8 /west/ ....
9 /ˈjeləʊ/ ....
10 /jɪə/ ....

(B66) Listen to check your answers. Check with the Key. Then listen and repeat.

23.2 Complete the dialogues using these words.

away	few	music	quarter	tunes	weather	Wednesday	weekend	west
wet	~~when~~	where	where	windy	yes	yesterday	yet	young

1 A: ....*When*....'s your interview?
B: It's on ...., at .... past one.
A: Good luck!

2 A: Are you going .... for the .... ?
B: ....
A: .... ?
B: I don't know ....

3 A: Hi! .... are you?
B: We're in .... Wales.
A: What's the .... like?
B: .... was .... and ....,
but today's beautiful.

4 A: Can you read .... ?
B: No, but I remember a ....
from when I was ....

(B67) Listen to check your answers. Check with the Key. Then listen and repeat.

23.3 Match the questions and answers in the interview.

Questions	*Answers*
What? A *wallet*	In the town square.
What colour?	Yellow.
With?	Twelve.
Where?	I was waiting in a queue. They were quick. They ran away.
When?	Yesterday.
What time?	Money, keys, cards – the usual things.
Who?	Two young men.
What happened?	~~A wallet.~~

Well, we'll see what we can do.

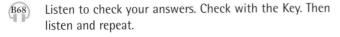

(B68) Listen to check your answers. Check with the Key. Then listen and repeat.

24 Sunglasses or umbrella?
Consonant groups in the middle of words

A (B69) Some words have one consonant sound in the middle. Listen.

paper
pepper (**pp** is 2 letters but only 1 sound)
weather (**th** is 2 letters but only 1 sound)
listen (**st** is 2 letters but only 1 sound – **t** is silent)

B (B70a) Some words have groups of two or three consonant sounds in the middle. Listen.

colder (**ld** is 2 sounds)
computer (**mp** is 2 sounds)
classroom (**ssr** is 2 sounds)
sixteen (**xt** is 3 sounds /kst/)

(B70b) Listen and repeat these words with two consonant sounds in the middle. Be careful – don't put a vowel sound between the consonants.

alphabet
asking
bookshop
building
dancing
lovely
remember
timetable

(B70c) Listen and repeat these words with three consonant sounds in the middle.

children
complete
country
downstairs
expensive
friendly
sunglasses
umbrella

(B70d)

Important for listening

Sometimes we don't pronounce all the consonant sounds clearly. Listen.

Se(p)tember	goo(d)bye
Chris(t)mas	brea(k)fast
pi(c)nic	foo(t)ball
pos(t)card	sho(p)keeper

Exercises

24.1 Complete the words.

1 The day after Monday is Tues day.
2 37 + 13 = fi_ _y
3 The opposite of cheap is e_ _ e_ _ive.
4 A very short distance: a ce_ _imetre.
5 Something to write with: a pe_ _il.
6 The last month of the year is Dece_ _er.
7 The month after August is Se_ _ember.
8 The room where you sleep is the be_ _oom.
9 The tenth month of the year is O_ _ober.
10 An important test is an e_am.

B71 Listen to check your answers. Check with the Key. Then listen and repeat.

24.2 Complete the words.

1 In winter we go skiing in the _ _ _nt _ _ _ _.
2 The hotel _ _ _ _pt_ _ _ is open 24 hours a day.
3 The road was closed yesterday because of an _cc_ _ _ _ _.
4 Don't forget to send me a _ _ stc _ _ _ from England.
5 Shall I take my _ _ngl_ _ _ _ _ or my _mbr_ _ _ _ ?

B72 Listen to check your answers. Check with the Key. Then listen and repeat.

24.3 Underline the consonant groups in the middle of words in the dialogues.

1 A: How's your English?
  B: I think I need to practise more – I have
     problems with making sentences, and tenses,
     and pronunciation, and listening, and answering
     questions, and conversation, and I make too
     many mistakes …
  A: Don't worry, it's not so bad! You're almost an
     expert!

2 A: Where's my passport?
  B: I don't know. In your suitcase, maybe?
  A: Where's my suitcase?
  B: Upstairs, in the wardrobe.
  A: Right. And where's the envelope that was on the
     kitchen table?
  B: In the wastepaper basket – was it important?

B73 Listen to check your answers. Check with the Key. Then
listen and repeat.

25 Train in the rain
Consonant groups at the beginning of words

A 🎧 B74 Some words have one consonant sound at the beginning. Listen.

late
rain
white   (**wh** is 2 letters but only 1 sound)

Some words have groups of two or three consonant sounds at the beginning. Listen and repeat these words. Be careful – don't put a vowel sound between the consonants.

B 🎧 B75a Two consonant sounds at the beginning:

plate
train
quite   (**qu** is pronounced /kw/)

🎧 B75b Three consonant sounds at the beginning:

spring
street
square   (**squ** is pronounced /skw/)

🎧 B75c Here are some more examples. Listen and repeat.

1	**br**ead	Pass me some **br**ead.
2	**pr**ice	What's the **pr**ice?
3	**bl**ess	*(sneeze)* **Bl**ess you!
4	**cl**ass	How many are there in your **cl**ass?
5	**gl**ass	Where are my **gl**asses?
6	**cr**eam	Do you like ice **cr**eam?
7	**qu**iet	Isn't it **qu**iet?
8	**sp**ell	How do you **sp**ell it?
9	**st**and	Where shall I **st**and?
10	**sw**im	Can you **sw**im?
11	**str**anger	I'm a **str**anger here.
12	**str**ess	a job with a lot of **str**ess

Bless you!

Exercises

25.1 Listen and circle the word you hear.

1	(dress)	address
2	rain	train
3	miles	smiles
4	cool	school
5	sleep	asleep
6	rain	train
7	dress	address
8	sleep	asleep
9	miles	smiles
10	cool	school
11	win	twin
12	win	twin

Check with the Key. Then listen again and repeat the sentences.

25.2 Make as many words as you can with sounds from boxes 1+2, 1+2+3 or 2+3.

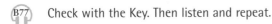

	box 1	box 2	box 3
	g r	eɪ	t
1	p l t r	eɪ	n t
2	f t θ s r	iː	t
3	s n l	əʊ	z p
4	f r l	aɪ	t

EXAMPLE *grey, great, gate, eight*

 Check with the Key. Then listen and repeat.

25.3 Complete the words. They all have two consonant sounds and two consonant letters.

1 I don't like travelling by p̲ ̲l̲ane.
2 The sky's _ _ue today.
3 What would you like to _ _ink?
4 Is it the _ _elfth today?
5 Is this seat _ _ee?
6 It's five o'_ _ock.
7 How many languages can you _ _eak?
8 Don't sit on that dirty _ _oor.

 Listen to check your answers. Check with the Key. Then listen and repeat.

I don't like travelling by plane.

26 Pink and orange
Consonant groups at the end of words

A B79a Some words have one consonant sound at the end. Listen.

sto**p**
si**ck** (**ck** is 2 letters but only 1 sound /k/)

B79b Some words have groups of two or three consonant sounds at the end. Listen.

sto**ps** (**ps** is 2 sounds)
sta**mp** (**mp** is 2 sounds)
si**x** (**x** is 1 letter but 2 sounds /ks/)
sta**mps** (**mps** is 3 sounds)
si**xth** (**xth** is 3 sounds /ksθ/)

B B80 Listen and repeat these words with two consonant sounds at the end. Be careful – don't put a vowel sound between the consonants.

arri**ved**
a**sk**
bui**ld**
da**nce**
fi**nd**
fini**shed**
he**lp**
sto**ps**
sta**mp**
si**x**

C B81a Listen and repeat these words with three consonant sounds at the end. Be careful – don't put a vowel sound between the consonants.

a**sks**
bui**lds**
cri**sps**
da**nced**
he**lps**
si**xth**
sta**mps**

B81b
Sometimes we don't pronounce all the consonant sounds clearly. Listen.

Important for listening

sto(p)s	hel(p)	frien(d)s
as(k)	stam(p)	wan(t)s
stam(p)s	hel(p)ed	buil(d)s

Exercises

26.1
(B82)

Listen and circle the word you hear.

1	(cold)	colder	6	old	older
2	cold	colder	7	sent	centre
3	dance	dancer	8	sent	centre
4	dance	dancer	9	fast	faster
5	old	older	10	fast	faster

Check with the Key. Then listen and repeat.

26.2
(B83)

Listen and complete the sentences with words from Exercise 26.1.

1 Yesterday was ....*cold*........ , but today's ....
2 My wife's a good .... but I can't .... at all.
3 I'm .... than you, but not too .... to learn English.
4 I .... my daughter to buy some things in the shopping ....
5 The bus is .... but the train's ....

Check with the Key. Then listen and repeat.

26.3

Underline the consonant groups at the ends of words in the dialogues.

1 A: Have you seen that fi<u>lm</u>? B: No, I haven't.
2 A: Be there at six. B: Is that when it starts?
3 A: Have you been to France? B: Yes, once.
4 A: How do you say 'Hello' in French? B: I can't speak French.
5 A: Have some of these biscuits. B: No, thanks, I don't like them.
6 A: I found some money in the street today. B: How much? A: Fifty pence.
7 A: What's for lunch? B: Fish and chips.
8 A: I only slept six hours last night. B: I didn't sleep at all!
9 A: What colour are your new gloves? B: Pink and orange!

(B84) Check with the Key. Then listen and repeat.

26.4

Complete each phrase with one of the words in the box.

boots	physics	west	silence
thousands	isn't	banks	~~last~~

EXAMPLE
   first and ....*last*........

1 maths and ....
2 it wasn't and it ....
3 hundreds and ....
4 socks and ....
5 shops and ....
6 sound and ....
7 from east to ....

(B85) Listen to check your answers. Check with the Key. Then listen and repeat.

27 Last week
Consonant groups across words

A 🎧 B86 Sometimes a word ends with a consonant or a consonant group, and the next word starts with a consonant or consonant group, and you pronounce the consonants together as a group. Listen and repeat.

this_time
a plane_ticket
a pop_star
an English_class
the next_word
orange_juice
this_morning
time_to go
an old_castle

A pop star   An old castle

🎧 B87 Sometimes you don't hear all the consonants clearly. Listen and repeat.

Important for listening

stop_the game	sto(p) the game
last_week	las(t) week
back_to work	ba(ck) to work
and_then ...	an(d) then ...
put your bag_down	put your ba(g) down

B 🎧 B88 Sometimes the sound of one of the consonants changes. Listen and repeat.

ten	ten_boys	(n sounds like **m**)
	ten_girls	(n sounds like /ŋ/)
goo**d**	good**b**ye	(**d** sounds like **b**)
	good_goal!	(**d** sounds like **g**)

Good goal!

C 🎧 B89 If the same consonant sound comes at the end of one word and the beginning of the next word, you usually hear it only once, but longer than normal. Listen and repeat.

ten_nights
this_summer
some_money
enough_food
stop_playing
a good_day
a black_cat
call_later

Exercises

27.1 Listen and complete the sentences.

(B90)

EXAMPLE

Were you at the .... *last* .... meeting?

1 See you .... week.
2 Have a .... time.
3 Have a .... holiday.
4 .... me a call.
5 .... me an email.
6 .... me how you are.
7 .... me a letter.
8 .... me a present.

Check with the Key. Then listen again and repeat.

27.2 Underline the consonant groups across words in these sentences.

It's really warm today.

EXAMPLE

This i<u>s the</u> la<u>st t</u>ime.

1 It's really warm today.
2 Try this sentence.
3 I don't know what to do.
4 Look through all the photos.
5 Check the answer.
6 I'd like to ask you something.
7 Is this the right place?
8 I haven't listened to this CD yet.
9 The meeting's on Monday.
10 The potatoes aren't cooked yet.

(B91) Listen to check your answers. Check with the Key. Then listen and repeat.

27.3 Complete the phrases with the words from the box. You will need to use some of them more than once.

~~this~~	young	cheap	white	big	next	black	last	old	small

.... *this* .... month   .... month   .... month
a/an .... town   a/an .... town   a/an .... town
a/an .... cat   a/an .... cat   a/an .... cat
a/an .... cat   a/an .... cat   a/an .... cat
.... clothes   .... clothes   .... clothes
.... clothes   .... clothes   .... clothes

(B92) Check with the Key. Then listen and repeat.

28 One house, two houses
Syllables

A C2a Listen to these three lists of words. The words in list 1 have three parts – we say they have three **syllables**. The words in list 2 have two syllables, and the words in list 3 have one syllable.

1	2	3
in-ter-net	six-ty	six
un-der-line	un-der	line
un-der-lined	u-nit	lines
al-pha-bet	hou-ses	house
con-so-nant	go-ing	goes

C2b Some words have more than three syllables: *television* has four syllables, for example, and *geographical* has five syllables. Listen.

te-le-vi-sion
ge-o-gra-phi-cal

C2c The simplest type of syllable is just a vowel sound, like /uː/. People often say the vowel sound /uː/ (usually written *Ooh*) when they are pleased or surprised. Listen.

Ooh, that's nice!
Ooh, thank you very much!

Ooh, thank you very much!

C2d Some syllables have one or more consonant sounds before the vowel. Listen.

/s/ + /uː/ = /suː/ This is the name *Sue*.
/bl/ + /uː/ = /bluː/ blue

C2e Some syllables have one or more consonants after the vowel. Listen.

/iː/ + /t/ = /iːt/ eat
/iː/ + /st/ = /iːst/ east

C2f Some syllables have consonants before and after the vowel. Listen.

/nj/ + /uː/ + /z/ = /njuːz/ news
/f/ + /iː/ + /ldz/ = /fiːldz/ fields
/str/ + /iː/ + /t/ = /striːt/ street

B C3a Usually, the number of syllables in a word is the number of vowel <u>sounds</u> – not the number of vowel <u>letters</u>. Listen.

w<u>or</u>k<u>e</u>d   (2 vowel letters but only 1 vowel sound /wɜːkt/, so only 1 syllable)
d<u>i</u>ff<u>e</u>r<u>e</u>nt   (3 vowel letters but only 2 vowel sounds /'dɪfrənt/, so only 2 syllables)
<u>i</u>nt<u>e</u>r<u>e</u>st<u>i</u>ng   (4 vowel letters but only 3 vowel sounds /'ɪntrəstɪŋ/, so only 3 syllables)

C3b Sometimes the sound /l/ can be a syllable with no vowel sound. Listen.

bottle   (2 syllables /'bɒ/ + /tl/)
syllable   (3 syllables /'sɪ/ + /lə/ + /bl/)
It'll be ready soon.   (2 syllables /ɪt/ + /l/)

Exercises

28.1 How many syllables are there in these words? Write the number of syllables next to the word.

eyes ☐1☐   why ☐   white ☐   write ☐   writing ☐   glass ☐   glasses ☐
university ☐   business ☐   information ☐

(C4a) Listen to check your answers. Check with the Key.

(C4b) Then listen and repeat these sentences.

1 I've got blue eyes.	6 Is this your glass?
2 I don't know why.	7 I don't wear glasses.
3 Black coffee or white?	8 Where's the university?
4 Will you write to me?	9 Business is business.
5 What are you writing?	10 There's the information office.

28.2
1 Which day of the week has three syllables?
2 How many syllables do the other days of the week have?
3 Which numbers between 1 and 20 have three syllables?
4 Which letter of the alphabet has more than one syllable?
5 Which months have only one syllable?

(C5) Listen to check your answers. Check with the Key. Then listen and repeat.

28.3 Read this story and mark all the words that have two or three syllables.

I remember(3) once on my first visit(2) to England( ), soon after( ) I started( ) learning( ) English( ), my landlady( ) went shopping( ) and she came back with a big bag full of things, but she forgot( ) to buy some soup – she needed( ) a tin of tomato( ) soup. So I said, 'I'll go to the shop and buy it for you,' because( ) I wanted( ) to be helpful( ) and it was a chance to practise( ) my English( ) a bit. So I went to the little( ) shop round the corner( ) and asked the shopkeeper( ) for tomato( ) soup. But he seemed surprised( ), he didn't( ) understand( ), and I repeated( ) again( ) and again( ) 'soup, tomato( ) soup' until( ) he gave me some red soap, and I realised( ) I'd confused( ) 'soup' and 'soap' and I was asking( ) for 'tomato( ) soap'. I felt terrible( ), I wanted( ) to run out of the shop, but my landlady( ) wanted( ) her soup, so I said, 'Thank you. And tomato( ) soup, please' – this time with the correct( ) pronunciation – and he gave me the soup. I paid and went back to the house and said to the landlady( ), pronouncing( ) very( ) carefully( ), 'Here's your soup, and I bought you this soap as a present( ),' and she said, 'Ooh, thank you very much, that's very( ) nice of you!'

(C6) Listen to check your answers. Check with the Key. Then listen and practise reading the story aloud.

29 Wait a minute – where's the waiter?
Strong and weak vowels

A C7a The word *London* has two vowel sounds that are written the same – **Lond_o_n** – but pronounced differently. The first **o** has a clear, strong sound, but the second **o** has a weak sound. Listen carefully to the difference.
London

C7b The word *banana* has three vowel sounds which are written the same – **b_a_nan_a_**. The second **a** has a clear, strong sound, but the first **a** and the third **a** have a weak sound. Listen.
banana

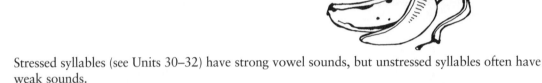

Stressed syllables (see Units 30–32) have strong vowel sounds, but unstressed syllables often have weak sounds.

The weak sound in Lond_o_n and b_a_nan_a_ is /ə/.
London /ˈlʌndən/
banana /bəˈnɑːnə/

C8a

Important for listening

Sometimes it's difficult to hear /ə/. Listen.

London
I have to go to London tomorrow.
banana
Would you like a banana?

This is very important for listening, because it makes it difficult to recognise words. When you speak English, you don't need to pronounce weak sounds as weakly as this, but it's important to make a clear difference between stressed (strong) and unstressed (weak) syllables.

C8b Listen to the other weak vowels in these two sentences.

```
W S   W S W S  W  W S W
I have to go to London tomorrow.
```
have – go – Lon – morr are strong, and the others are weak.

```
 W   W S  W W S W
Would you like a banana?
```
like – na are strong, and the others are weak.

B Sometimes different words sound the same because of the weak vowels. Look at these three sentences.
Where's the waiter?
Is this the way to the school?
Can you wait a minute?

waiter, way to and **wait a** sound the same: /ˈweɪtə/.

C9 Listen to the three sentences and repeat.

Exercises

29.1 In the words below, * represents the weak vowel /ə/. Write the words with their full spelling.

EXAMPLE

lett*   letter

1 Brit*n ....   5 *noth* ....

2 t*day ....   6 *gain ....

3 *meric* ....   7 mount*n ....

4 p*lice ....

C10a Listen to check your answers. Check with the Key.

C10b Then listen and repeat these phrases.

1 Great Brit*n   5 have *noth*

2 arriving t*day   6 say it *gain

3 going to *meric*   7 climb the mount*n

4 call th* p*lice

29.2 Look at the sentences below and find words and phrases in list 1 and list 2 with the same pronunciation.

EXAMPLE

Where's the <u>waiter</u>? – Can you <u>wait a</u> minute?

Where's the waiter?

list 1	list 2
~~Where's the waiter?~~	I heard a loud noise.
Not at all.	You'll see a tall building on your left.
Look in the cellar.	My father knew a lot about music.
It takes a long time.	~~Can you wait a minute?~~
Smoking isn't allowed.	I'm trying to sell a house.
I'd like to live in a newer house.	Walk along the beach.

C11 Listen to check your answers. Check with the Key. Then listen and repeat.

29.3 Write these words.

EXAMPLE

/prəˈnaʊns/ pronounce

1 /əˈmerɪkə/ ....   5 /təˈdeɪ/ ....

2 /ˈsentəns/ ....   6 /ˈletə/ ....

3 /ˈdɪfrənt/ ....   7 /pəˈliːs/ ....

4 /ˈmaʊntən/ ....   8 /əˈgen/ ....

C12 Check with the Key. Then listen and repeat.

30 Single or return?
Stress in two-syllable words

A

C13a In a two-syllable word, one syllable is stronger than the other. This is the **stressed** syllable. In the word *answer* the first syllable is stressed. (We also say: 'The **stress** is on the first syllable.') Listen.

answer

C13b In the word *again* the second syllable is stressed. (The stress is on the second syllable.) Listen.

a**gain**

C13c Two-syllable words often have stress on the first syllable, and the vowel sound in the unstressed syllable is often the weak sound /ə/. Listen and repeat.

brother   **butt**er   **fath**er   **fing**er   **fin**ish   **glass**es   **lis**ten   **moth**er   **num**ber   **sec**ond
sister   **wat**er   **wo**man

C13d Sometimes there's no vowel sound in the unstressed syllable. Listen and repeat.

apple   **peo**ple   **sim**ple   **ta**ble   **trav**el

C13e Some two-syllable words are stressed on the second syllable. Listen and repeat.

a**gree**   a**lone**   a**rrive**   a**sleep**   a**wake**
be**cause**   be**gin**   be**hind**
com**plete**
de**cide**
ex**am**   ex**plain**   ex**press**
per**haps**   pro**nounce**
re**peat**   re**turn**

B

We can show stressed syllables like this O, and unstressed syllables like this o. So words like *answer*, *brother*, *butter* look like this Oo, and words like *again*, *because*, *decide* look like this oO.

Dictionaries usually show stress with this sign ˈ in front of the stressed syllable.

answer   /ˈɑːnsə/
again   /əˈgen/

Exercises

30.1 Listen and circle the word with different stress.

C14

EXAMPLE

oO	oO	oO	Oo
exam	excuse	explain	(extra)

1 actor	after	afraid	also
2 before	belong	better	between
3 paper	pencil	picture	police

4 coffee	colour	concert	correct
5 English	enjoy	evening	every

Check your answers with the Key. Listen and underline the stressed syllables. Then listen again and repeat.

30.2 Make words from these parts and write them in the correct column.

a   **re**   **long**   **ing**   **er**   **sleep**
  turn

words with first-syllable stress	words with second-syllable stress
.......longer.......	....
....	....
....	....

C15   Check your answers with the Key. Then listen and repeat.

30.3 All these phrases have five syllables. O is a stressed syllable and o is an unstressed syllable. Put the phrases in the correct place.

~~teacher or student?~~   the same or different?
single or return?   behind or in front?
asleep or awake?   perhaps or maybe?
finish or begin?   reading or writing?

OooOo 1 ....teacher or student?.......
      2 ....

OoooO 1 ....
      2 ....

oOoOo 1 ....
      2 ....

oOooO 1 ....
      2 ....

C16   Listen to check your answers. Check with the Key. Then listen and repeat.

30.4 Put the stress mark ˈ in the correct place and write the word.

EXAMPLE

/əraɪv/ → /əˈraɪv/ ....arrive.......

1 /sɪstə/ ....
2 /rɪlæks/ ....
3 /piːpl/ ....

4 /fɪnɪʃ/ ....
5 /kəmpliːt/ ....
6 /teɪbl/ ....
7 /prənaʊns/ ....

C17   Listen to check your answers. Check with the Key. Then listen and repeat.

31

Begin at the beginning
Stress in longer words

A C18 Some words have more than two syllables. In every word, one syllable is stressed. Listen and repeat. O is the stressed syllable and oo the unstressed syllables.

Ooo
exercise   **syll**able   There are three syllables in the word *exercise*.

oOo
com**put**er   ex**am**ple   *Computer* is an example of a three-syllable word.

ooO
under**stand**   Japa**nese**   I can't understand Japanese.

Oooo
supermarket   Do you like small shops or supermarkets?

oOoo
pho**to**graphy   Are you interested in photography?

ooOo
infor**ma**tion   mathe**ma**tics   I'd like some information about mathematics courses.

oOooo
vo**ca**bulary   Will you help me with my vocabulary?

ooOoo
uni**ver**sity   Which university did you go to?

oooOo
communi**ca**tion   Email is very helpful for communication.

B C19a When you add syllables to words, the stress often stays on the same syllable. Listen and repeat.

be**gin**	→	be**ginn**ing
de**cide**	→	de**cid**ed
possible	→	im**po**ssible
sentence	→	**sen**tences
interest	→	**in**teresting

C19b But sometimes a different syllable is stressed. Listen and repeat.

e**lec**tric	→	elec**tri**city
pro**nounce**	→	pronun**ci**ation
photograph	→	pho**to**graphy
ex**plain**	→	expla**na**tion

Exercises

31.1 Write these words.

EXAMPLE /bɪ'ɡɪnɪŋ/   <u>beginning</u>
1 /'ɪntəvjuː/ ....
2 /mjuː'ziːəm/ ....
3 /mæɡə'ziːn/ ....
4 /'defɪnətli/ ....
5 /ə'merɪkən/ ....
6 /pɒlɪ'tɪʃən/ ....
7 /næʃə'næləti/ ....
8 /fə'tɒɡrəfi/ ....

C20 Listen to check your answers. Check with the Key. Then listen and repeat.

31.2 Listen and write the words in the correct column.

C21a

~~adjective~~ alphabet cinema eleven furniture grandmother important
reception remember tomorrow

Ooo   **oOo**
<u>adjective</u>   ....
....
....
....
....

C21b Check your answers with the Key. Then listen and repeat.

31.3 Complete the sentences. Choose words with the correct stress from the box. You do not need all the words.

afternoon bicycle conversation ~~delicious~~ discussion exercises expensive
holiday morning normally often Saturday seventeen seventy sixty
Sunday Sweden Switzerland telephone today yesterday

1 We had a oOo <u>delicious</u> meal on Ooo ....
2 We Ooo .... go on Ooo .... by car, but this time we're going by Ooo
....
3 I did ten grammar Oooo .... Ooo ....
4 Is Ooo .... an oOo .... country?
5 My son's ooO .... and my father's Ooo ....
6 I had a long Ooo .... ooOo .... this ooO ....

C22 Listen to check your answers. Check with the Key. Then listen and repeat.

31.4 Six months of the year have three or four syllables. Write them on the correct line.

Oooo   ....
oOo   <u>September</u>   ....

C23 Listen to check your answers. Check with the Key. Then listen and repeat.

32 Where's my checklist?
Stress in compound words

A

We can often put two words together to make a **compound**, e.g. class + room → classroom.
We write some compounds as one word, some as two words, and some with a hyphen (-).

class + room → classroom
car + park → car park
second + hand → second-hand

C24 The stress is normally on the first part of the compound. Listen and repeat.

Oo	**air**port **bath**room **bus** stop **car** park **class**room **foot**ball **girl**friend
Ooo	**bus** station **din**ing room **hair**dresser **news**paper **post** office **sun**glasses
Oooo	**pho**tocopy **rail**way station **shop** assistant
oOoo	po**lice** station
oOooo	com**pu**ter programme

B

C25a Some compound nouns have stress on both parts if the first part is an adjective. Listen and repeat.

OoO   sing**le room**

C25b Some compound nouns have stress on both parts if the thing in the second part is made of the material in the first part. Listen and repeat.

OO	**glass jar**
OoO	**plas**tic **bag**
oOoO	to**ma**to **soup**

C25c Some compound nouns have stress on both parts if the first part tells us where the second part is. Listen and repeat.

OO	**car door front door ground floor**
OoOo	**ci**ty **cen**tre **kit**chen **win**dow

C25d When a compound is an adjective, there is often stress on both parts. Listen and repeat.

OO	**first-class half-price home-made**
OoO	**se**cond-**hand**

Exercises

32.1 Listen and circle the compound with different stress. In the example, both words are stressed in *back door*, but in the others, the first word is stressed.

EXAMPLE

computer screen   (back door)   alarm clock   bank manager
1 toothache   night club   crossroads   half-price
2 motorbike   waiting room   second class   traffic lights
3 mobile phone   credit card   swimming pool   check-in desk
4 travel agent   city centre   tourist visa   supermarket

32.2 Make five compounds from these parts.

first part:	ear wine hand birthday boy
second part:	friend bar present bag rings

....

Now use the compounds to complete the dialogue.

A: Oh no, I can't find my ....!
B: Have you looked in your ....?
A: Of course!
B: Maybe you left them in that .... last night?
A: Oh no, maybe I did!
B: Are they important?
A: Yes – they were a .... from my ....!

Listen to check your answers. Check with the Key. Listen again and circle the stressed part of each compound. Then listen again and repeat.

32.3 Listen to the poem. The compounds are underlined. Circle the stressed part of each compound.

Checklist
Have I ...
... set the (alarm) clock?
... and put it on the bedside table?
... put my plane ticket in my trouser pocket?
... packed my toothbrush?
... put my suitcase by the bedroom door?
... switched the CD player off?
... phoned the taxi driver to say 'Be here at six'?
Have I ...
Have I ...
... Where's my checklist?!

Check your answers with the Key. Then listen again and repeat.

33 Phrases and pauses
Reading aloud

A

When you listen to English, perhaps you think it's difficult to understand because it's too fast. And perhaps you would like to speak faster. But when people speak English – or any other language – they don't speak fast and non-stop. They speak in short phrases, and they stop, or pause, between the phrases.

B

First, read this story, and make sure you understand it.

> Lots of people get arrested for dangerous driving, of course. But how old is the oldest? Who's the world record holder? Well, I read about a man who was a hundred and four! He went through red lights, crashed into parked cars and drove along the pavement. And how old was his car? Only thirty.

C29a Now listen to the story, reading at the same time, and notice the pauses between the lines.

> Lots of people get arrested for dangerous driving,
> of course.
> But how old is the oldest?
> Who's the world record holder?
> Well,
> I read about a man
> who was a hundred and four!
> He went through red lights,
> crashed into parked cars
> and drove along the pavement.
> And how old was his car?
> Only thirty.

C29b It's OK – or even better – to pause more often, because it gives you more time to think of what to say next, and it makes listening easier. Listen to this version – the words are the same, but there are more pauses.

> Lots of people
> get arrested
> for dangerous driving,
> of course.
> But
> how old
> is the oldest?
> Who's the world record holder?
> Well,
> I read about a man
> who was
> a hundred and four!
> He went through red lights,
> crashed into parked cars
> and drove along the pavement.
> And how old was his car?
> Only thirty.

C29b It's also important to stress the most important words. Listen again, and this time notice the stress on the words in **bold**.

> **Lots** of people
> get ar**rest**ed
> for **dan**gerous **driv**ing,
> of **course**.
> **But**
> **how old**
> is the **old**est?
> **Who's** the **world rec**ord holder?
> **Well**,
> I read about a **man**
> who was
> a **hun**dred and **four**!
> He **went** through **red lights**,
> **crashed** into **parked cars**
> and **drove** along the **pave**ment.
> And **how old** was his **car**?
> **On**ly **thir**ty.

Practise reading this story, phrase by phrase, paying attention to the pauses and the stresses.

Exercises

33.1 Listen to this story and mark the pauses like this: / .

A few years ago / I read in a newspaper / that the staff at a library ...

A few years ago I read in a newspaper that the staff at a library in a small town in the west of England had noticed that the number of visitors to the library was going down and down, and the number of books they were borrowing was going down even faster. They couldn't understand this, so they decided to do some research to find out the reason. They interviewed people and asked them to fill in questionnaires and so on. And guess what they discovered. The reason was simply that everybody had read all the books already!

Check with the Key.

Listen again and mark the main stresses by underlining them.

A few <u>years</u> ago / I read in a <u>news</u>paper / that the staff at a <u>lib</u>rary ...

Check with the Key and practise reading the story yourself. You could also practise reading together with the recording.

33.2 Listen to this story and mark the pauses.

This seems unbelievable but it's a true story in fact. A farmer was working in the fields with his tractor. The tractor crashed and he fell out and landed on the ground unconscious. As he fell, his mobile phone fell out of his pocket. Soon after, a bird that was flying around the fields saw the phone and started pecking it with its beak. Amazingly it dialled the number 999 and soon the emergency services arrived to help the farmer.

Check with the Key.

Listen again and mark the main stresses.

Check with the Key and practise reading the story yourself. You could also practise reading together with the recording.

Tip: You might find it helpful to rewrite the stories with each phrase on a separate line, like this:
A few <u>years</u> ago
I read in a <u>newspaper</u>
that the staff at a <u>library</u> ...

 Note: When we write, we mark some of the main pauses with commas, like this:
This seems unbelievable, but it's a true story, in fact.

34 Speak it, write it, read it
Linking words together 1

A

When we write there are spaces between all the words, but when we speak we link a lot of the words together, so it sounds like this: *whenwespeakwelinkalotofthewordstogether*.

C32a Listen and notice how a consonant sound at the end of a word is linked to a vowel sound at the start of the next word.

Look_at that! Breakfast_in bed!
A: Bought_it? B: No, caught_it!
That's_enough! Switch_it_off!

Now say the sentences, making the same links.

C32b Of course, we can also separate the words if we want to. Listen to the difference.

I said <u>switch</u> … <u>it</u> … <u>off</u>!!!

Breakfast in bed!

Bought it?

Switch it off!

B

Listen and repeat these poems.

C33a **English**
Speak_it
Write_it
Read_it
You know
you really
need_it!

C33b **Don't forget**
First you close_it
Then you lock_it
And put the key back_in your pocket.

C33c **Busy**
Work_all day
Run_away
Boss_and me
Can't_agree
Fill_a cup
Drink_it_up
Wait_a while
Walk_a mile
Meet_at_eight
Don't be late!

C34a Important for listening
• The letter **h** at the beginning of *he, his, her* and *him* is often not pronounced (see Unit 37) so the first sound in these words is often a vowel sound. Listen.

Can we go back? My husband's forgotten_(h)is passport.
A: Where's the boss? B: I don't know, I haven't seen_(h)er.

C34b • Where there's a /t/ sound before a vowel, some people don't pronounce the /t/ clearly. Listen.

switch_i(t) off   drink_i(t) up   can'(t) agree

Exercises

34.1 Mark where you think there will be links between consonants and vowels.

1 Choose the correct_answer and tick it.
2 Which page is it on?
3 How do you spell it?
4 How do you pronounce it?
5 What does it mean?
6 I can't understand this.
7 Look it up in your dictionary.
8 It isn't easy to speak English.
9 Listen – which language is that?
10 Don't worry if you make a mistake.

C35 Listen to check your answers. Check with the Key. Then listen and repeat.

34.2 Complete the sentences with the correct forms of the verbs.

EXAMPLE A: How did you feel?
B: I ___felt___ (feel) all right.

1 A: What do you think of yoga?
B: I don't know, I've never _____ (try) it.
2 A: What happened to my favourite cup?
B: It _____ (fall) off the table.
3 A: Which film shall we go to?
B: I don't mind. I've _____ (see) all of
them before.
4 A: You look pleased.
B: Yes, I've _____ (find) a new job.
5 A: What did you do last night?
B: I just _____ (stay) at home.
6 A: Where did you buy that hat?
B: I _____ (make) it myself!
7 A: Does your dog like biscuits?
B: I don't know, I've never _____ (ask) it.
8 A: How did you get here?
B: I _____ (swim) across the river.

Where did you buy that hat?

C36 Listen to check your answers. Check with the Key. Then listen and repeat. Be sure to link the final consonant of the verb with the vowel at the beginning of the next word.

34.3 Circle the /r/ sounds that you think will be pronounced. (See Unit 22.)

1 Where are you going?
2 Where shall we go?
3 Where did I put my scissors?
4 I don't know where I put my scissors.
5 Have another biscuit.
6 Have another apple.
7 They're all coming with us.
8 They're coming with us.
9 Are you sure?
10 Are you sure about that?

C37 Listen to check your answers. Check with the Key. Then listen and repeat. If there's an /r/ sound before a vowel, link the /r/ and the vowel.

Me and you, you and me
Linking words together 2

A

We use the sounds /j/ and /w/ to link a vowel sound at the end of a word with a vowel sound at the beginning of the next word.

C38a If the first word ends with a vowel sound like /ɪ/ or /iː/, and the next word starts with any vowel sound, we use /j/ to link the words. Listen.

me ʲand you
three ʲor four
the ʲend

C38b If the first word ends with a vowel sound like /ʊ/ or /uː/, and the next word starts with any vowel sound, we use /w/ to link the words. Listen.

you ʷand me
two ʷor three
go ʷoutside

B

Listen and repeat these poems.

C39a **Asking the way**
Yes.
Go ʷout of the building.
Go ʷalong the street.
Go ʷover the bridge.
Go ʷacross the street.
Go ʷup the hill.
Take the ʲeighth street on your left.
And the ʲeleventh on your right.
Then …
… I'm not sure –
You'll have to ʷask again.

C39b **Hats**
I'll do ʷone for you
I'll give you ʷone too
a nice one
a new ʷone
a yellow ʷand blue ʷone.

C40

Important for listening

The letter **h** at the beginning of *he*, *his*, *her* and *him* is often not pronounced (see Unit 37), so the first sound in these words is often a vowel sound. Listen.

He can't come out tonight. He's got to do ʷ(h)is homework.
A: I'm afraid the boss is busy. B: When can I see ʲ(h)er?

Exercises

35.1 Listen and complete the dialogues. Then mark the /j/ and /w/ links.

(C41)

1 A: _Do you ͜ʷoften_ go swimming? B: Not really, I _____ or twice a month.
2 A: What's _____ letter in the alphabet? B: Maybe it's G or H _____?
3 A: When do _____ holiday? B: We _____ July or August.
4 A: What's your _____? B: Twenty-eight, Sea Avenue.
5 A: Try _____ soon. B: OK, I'll send you my answer _____.
6 A: Look! There's _____ the mountains. B: Really? I can't _____.

Check with the Key. Then listen and repeat.

35.2 Mark where you think there will be /j/ and /w/ links between words.

1 Is it blue ͜ʷor grey?
2 What day is it today?
  Thursday or Friday?
3 Coffee or tea?
4 Where's my interview
  suit?
5 Play a song for me.
6 Hello. Reception?
  Which city is this?
7 See you in the evening.
8 Why do we always
  have to get up so
  early?

(C42) Listen to check your answers. Check with the Key. Then listen and repeat.

35.3 Complete the answers to the questions and mark all the /j/ and /w/ links in the dialogues.

1 A: Are you the new assistant? B: Yes, I _____.
2 A: Is he in the same class as you? B: No, he _____.
3 A: Am I late? B: No, you _____. Come in.
4 A: Is she coming with us? B: Yes, she _____.
5 A: These chairs aren't very comfortable, are they? B: No, they _____.

(C43) Listen to check your answers. Check with the Key. Then listen and repeat.

36 Take me to the show, Jo
Rhythm

A C44 Stressed and unstressed syllables in words make different rhythms. Listen.

Oo   answer
oO   belong
Ooo   interview
oOo   banana

B Phrases have a rhythm of stressed and unstressed syllables, like words.

C45a Listen and repeat these words and phrases with this rhythm: Ooo

interview
telephone
talk to me
told you so
doesn't it?

C45b Listen and repeat these words and phrases with this rhythm: oOo

important
discussion
I told you
I'd like to
pronounce it

C45c Listen and repeat these words and phrases with this rhythm: ooOo

photographic
information
forty-seven
what about it?
never tried it

C45d Listen and repeat these phrases with this rhythm: OooO

time to get up
making mistakes
tell me again
give me your hand
twenty years old

Exercises

36.1 Read the phrases. Then listen and write 1 if the phrase has the pattern OoOo, and 2 if it has the
C46a pattern OooO.

what's the matter? 1	what shall we do? 2	stand in the queue
what about you?	see you later	tell the others
feeling better	nothing to do	come for dinner
anyone there?	round the corner	ready to go
on the TV	two and a half	go and find it
asking for more	what's the problem?	now and again
one pound forty	leave it to me	half a kilo
sixty-seven	breakfast's ready	quarter to four

C46b Check with the Key. Then listen and repeat.

36.2 Listen to this chant with this rhythm: oooOO. Write in the missing words.
C47

Pass me the ...._jam_......., Pam
Wait in the queue, Sue
See you ...., Jen
Leave it to me, Lee
What would you ...., Mike?
When shall we meet, Pete?
Over the ...., Bill
Where have you gone, John?

Soon as you ...., Van
Almost forgot, Scott
Lend me your ...., Ben
Where shall we go, Flo?
Get a new ...., Bob
How do you feel, Neil?
What have you ...., Dot?

Check with the Key. Then listen again and repeat.

36.3 Listen to this chant with this rhythm: ooooOO. Write in the missing words.
C48

Take me to the ...._show_......., Jo
Thank you for the food, Jude
See you in the ...., Mark
Really like the hat, Pat
See you on the ...., Jane

When will you be back, Jack?
Always on the ...., Joan
When did you arrive, Clive?
Have a glass of ...., Bruce.

Check with the Key. Then listen again and repeat.

36.4 Listen and repeat these poems. Be careful to say them with the right rhythm.

C49a **Too late**
Before I go –
I told you so
I told you,
but you still don't know.

C49c **Travel**
Heavy, light
The left and the right
I follow my feet
Through the day and the night.

C49b **Meeting**
Really can't wait
It's never too late
Quarter to eight?
That would be great.

C49d **Concentration**
Central station
Information
Trying to make a reservation
Not too keen on conversation
Don't want any complications.

Travel

A

Some words have two different pronunciations – a strong form and a weak form. Normally we use the weak form, but if the word is stressed because it is especially important, or because we want to show a contrast, we use the strong form. Most pronouns have strong and weak forms.

	weak	strong
you	/jə/	/juː/
me	/mɪ/	/miː/
he	/ɪ/	/hiː/
she	/ʃɪ/	/ʃiː/
him	/ɪm/	/hɪm/
her	/ə/ or /hə/*	/hɜː/*
we	/wɪ/	/wiː/
us	/əs/	/ʌs/
them	/ðəm/	/ðem/

* The **r** at the end of *her* is pronounced before a vowel (see Unit 22).
Give her‿a chance.

B Listen to the difference, and repeat.

A: Will you be at the meeting on Friday? (**you** is weak)
B: Yes. Will you be there? (**you** is strong)

Can you help me carry this suitcase? (**me** is weak)

Hey, wait for me! (**me** is strong)

A: Is he there? (**he** is weak)
B: Who?
A: The boss.
B: No. Everybody else is working, but he's gone home! (**he** is strong)

A: She doesn't smoke or drink! (**she** is strong)
B: Ah, that's what she told you! (**she** is weak)

A: Look – it's him! (**him** is strong)
B: Where? I can't see him. (**him** is weak)

A: Do you know that woman?
B: Her? No, I don't recognise her. (first **her** is strong, second **her** is weak)

A: I'm afraid we can't stay any longer. (**we** is weak)
B: What do you mean, 'we'? I've got plenty of time. (**we** is strong)

A: They told us to go this way. (**us** is weak)
B: Well, they didn't tell us! (**us** is strong)

When I said, 'Give them a drink' I didn't mean them, I meant the people. (first **them** is weak, second **them** is strong)

She doesn't smoke or drink.

They told us to go this way.

When I said, 'Give them a drink', I didn't mean them, I meant the people.

Exercises

37.1
C51

Listen and mark the underlined words *w* (weak) or *s* (strong).

1 A: Are you(w) going to talk to him(w)? B: No, I think he should talk to me first.
2 A: Shall I phone her? B: Yes, I think you should.
3 A: You see those people over there? Do you know them? B: I know her, but I don't know him.
4 A: What are you going to give him? B: I think I'll give him a shirt. What about you?
5 Let him come in and ask him what he wants.
6 She says she'll bring her money tomorrow.
7 I'm tired ... shall we go now?
8 Everybody's leaving. What about us? Shall we go, too?
9 Tell us when you're ready.
10 A: Who broke that window? B: He did! C: No, I didn't, she did!

Check with the Key. Then listen again and repeat.

37.2
C52

Listen and complete the sentences.

EXAMPLE
What ....*did she*.... say?
1 What .... think about it?
2 Where .... tonight?
3 .... ready .... now.
4 Where ....?
5 .... come in.
6 .... feeling all right?
7 Tell ....
8 I .... phone number but not ....

Check with the Key. Then listen again and repeat.

37.3
C53

Listen and repeat this poem. Be careful to speak with the correct rhythm. Stress the words in **bold**, and use weak forms of the pronouns between them.

Comings and goings

	What	did she	**say?**
Don't	**send**	her	a**way**
	Give	her a	**chance**
	Ask	her to	**dance**
	Give	us a	**drink**
	What	do you	**think?**
	Ask	them to	**wait**
	Tell	them it's	**late**
	What	shall we	**do?**
Shall we	**wait**	here for	**you?**
	Please	don't	de**lay**
Tell me,	**what**	do you	**say?**

And what's his name?
Strong and weak forms 2:
Possessives, conjunctions, prepositions

A

Many possessives, conjunctions and prepositions have two different pronunciations – a strong form and a weak form. Normally we use the weak form, but if the word is stressed because it is especially important, or because we want to show a contrast, we use the strong form.

	weak	strong
your	/jə/ *	/jɔː/ *
his	/ɪz/	/hɪz/
their	/ðə/ *	/ðeə/ *
and	/n/ or /ən/	/ænd/
but	/bət/	/bʌt/
some	/səm/	/sʌm/
that	/ðət/	/ðæt/
at	/ət/	/æt/
for	/fə/ *	/fɔː/ *
from	/frəm/	/frɒm/
of	/əv/	/ɒv/
to **	/tə/	/tʊ/

* The **r** at the end of these words is pronounced before a vowel (see Unit 22).
What's your‿address?
What was their‿answer?
Come in for‿a minute.

****to** is pronounced /tuː/ before a vowel sound.
to‿a party

B (C54) Listen to the difference, and repeat.

Give me your hand! (**your** is weak)

A: Your turn! (**your** is strong)
B: No, it's your turn! (**your** is strong)

A: That's our new neighbour.
B: And what's his name? (**and** and **his** are weak)
A: No, her! (**her** is strong)
B: Oh, sorry. What's her name? (**her** is strong)

A: She must be rich – look at her car! (**her** is weak)
B: I think that's his car, actually! (**his** is strong)

A: They've sold their old house, I see. (**their** is weak)
B: They've sold their house, yes, but they haven't bought another one yet. (**their** is strong)

A: Would you like some ice cream or some cake? (**some** is weak)
B: I'd like some ice cream and some cake, please! (**and** is strong, **some** is weak)

A: Do you like those sweets? (**do** and **you** are weak)
B: Well, some of them are good. (**some** is strong, **of** and **them** are weak)

The shop's closed from one to two. (**from** and **to** are weak)

There's a bus to the village at six, but there's no bus back from there tonight. (**to** and **from** are strong, **at** is weak)

Your turn!

She must be rich – look at her car!

Exercises

38.1 Listen and mark the underlined words *w* (weak) or *s* (strong).

                                    w

1 They went out <u>and</u> left <u>their</u> children <u>at</u> home.
2 Don't sit there – that's <u>his</u> seat.
3 Is this the train <u>to</u> London or <u>from</u> London?
4 I didn't say <u>at</u> five o'clock, I said about five o'clock.
5 What <u>are</u> you going <u>to</u> do?
6 <u>His</u> first name's Jack, but I don't know <u>his</u> second name.
7 Would you like <u>some</u> more tea?
8 Bring <u>your</u> umbrella – it's going <u>to</u> rain.
9 Excuse me – is this <u>your</u> umbrella?
10 Can you go <u>and</u> buy <u>some</u> bread <u>and</u> milk, please?
11 You've bought <u>some</u> flowers – who are they <u>for</u>?
12 I bought <u>them</u> <u>for</u> <u>you</u>!

Check with the Key. Then listen again and repeat.

38.2 Read and listen to these poems. Then listen again and repeat. Be careful to speak with the correct rhythm.

Use the weak form of *and*.

You and me
you and me
cake and tea
bread and cheese
twos and threes
this and that
thin and fat
left and right
day and night
now and then
where and when

Use the weak form of *of*.

Relaxing
a cup of tea
a new CD
a bottle of wine
and plenty of time

Use the weak form of *but*.

Making plans
A walk? But it's too late.
To the town? But it's too far.
Some sightseeing? But it's too dark.
A restaurant? But it's too expensive.
A game of chess? But it's so boring.
Read a book? But my eyes are so tired.
Study some English? But it's so difficult.
But let's do something. OK, what?

Use the weak form of *at*.

I remember it well
We met at a conference.
Or maybe at a party.
A party at a hotel.
Or perhaps at someone's house.
It was at lunchtime.
No, it was late at night.
Yes, and you were sitting at a table.
Or maybe standing at a window.
You looked at me and smiled.
No, you looked at me and laughed at me.
Yes, I remember it well.

Use the weak form of *your*.

A change of plan
Eat your sandwich.
Drink your tea.
Comb your hair.
Brush your teeth.
Put your shoes on.
Pack your bag.
Get your keys.
Ready?
What do you mean, you've changed your mind?

Making plans

39

There's a spider
Strong and weak forms 3: Articles, comparatives, 'there'

A C57a Some words have two different pronunciations – a strong form and a weak form. We normally use the weak forms of the words *a* and *an*. We say /ə/ before consonant sounds and /ən/ before vowel sounds. Listen and repeat.

a cup of coffee, please
a piece of cake, please
a lot of visitors
a Thursday morning in November
an invitation to a party
an umbrella in the rain

C57b Notice that some words begin with the vowel <u>letter</u> **u** but the consonant <u>sound</u> /j/, so we say *a* before them. Listen and repeat.

a university
a useful present

B C58 In comparatives, we use the weak forms of *than* /ðən/ and *as* /əz/, and we pronounce the ending *-er* as the weak vowel /ə/. Listen and repeat.

The new computer's better than the old one.
The old computer wasn't as good as the new one.

C C59a In the expressions *there's* and *there are* we normally use the weak form /ðə/. We pronounce *there's* as /ðəz/ and *there are* as /ðərə/. Listen and repeat.

There's a bridge over the river.
There are ten millimetres in a centimetre.

C59b But when we use the word *there* to talk about a place, we use the strong form /ðeə/. Listen and repeat.

A: Where are my glasses? B: Over there!

Over there!

Exercises

39.1
C60a
Listen and circle the mistakes in the picture (there are five mistakes).

C60b
Check with the Key. Then listen again and repeat.

39.2
C61
Listen and circle all the /ə/ sounds.

There's a cat on the mat.
There's a fish in a dish.
There's a dog in the fog,
and a mouse in the house.

There's a film on TV.
You can sit on my knee.
There are two cups of tea.
One for you, one for me.

Check with the Key.
Then listen again and repeat.

39.3
Complete the sentences using the words in the box. You will need to use some of them more than once.

tall	there	there's	there are	older	longer	as	than

1 Tessa's taller ....*than*.... Terry, but she isn't .... Ted.
  Ted's .... Tessa, but he isn't .... old .... Terry.
2 A: What's the longest tunnel in the world?
  B: The Channel Tunnel, between England and France?
  A: No, ... a .... one .... that.
  B: Is ...., really?
  A: Yes, ... is, in Japan.
3 A: How many dollars are .... in a pound?
  B: I think .... about one and a half ... or maybe .... one and a half pounds in a dollar?

Ted   Tessa   Terry

I am 109   I am 108   I am 110

C62
Listen to check your answers. Check with the Key. Then listen again and repeat.

39.4
C63
Listen and mark the underlined words *w* (weak) or *s* (strong).

A: What <u>are you</u> doing <u>there</u>?   *(w above "are you")*
B: <u>There</u>'s a spider in the room.
A: Is <u>there</u>? Where?
B: <u>There</u>, look!
A: No, <u>there</u> isn't!
B: Yes, <u>there</u> is!
A: Well, actually, <u>there</u> <u>are</u> two – one <u>there</u> <u>and</u> one <u>there</u>!

Check with the Key. Then listen and repeat.

40

Who was that?
Strong and weak forms 4: Auxiliary verbs

We often use the weak forms of these verbs:

| am | is | are | was | were | have | has | do | does | can | could |

C64 Listen and repeat.

1 I'm ready.
2 It's raining again.
3 Are you coming?
4 You're coming, aren't you?
5 Who was that?
6 The shops were all closed.

7 What have you got in your hand?
8 Has the programme started?
9 What do you want for Christmas?
10 Where does your sister live?
11 You can stay here if you like.
12 Could you spell your name for me, please?

C65 But if one of these verbs is stressed because it is especially important, or because we want to show a contrast, we use the strong form. Listen and repeat.

1 A: Are you ready? B: Yes, I am.
2 A: It isn't raining, is it? B: Yes, it is.
3 A: I'm not very good at English. B: Of course you are!
4 A: Is your father a teacher? B: He was, but he's retired now.
5 A: How many people are there in your class … ten? B: There were ten, but one left last week.
6 A: Have we met before? B: I don't think we have.
7 A: Has it started? B: Yes, come on, it has!
8 A: I don't like this music. B: Oh, I do.
9 A: Does the supermarket open on Sundays? B: I think it does.
10 A: I can't open this door. B: Let me try. Maybe I can.
11 A: Can you play tennis? B: Not now. I could when I was younger.

For more about *I'm*, *you're* and *it's*, see Unit 41.

Is your father a teacher?

Have we met before?

Exercises

40.1 Listen, and notice the weak forms underlined.

> It w̲a̲s̲ winter. It w̲a̲s̲ late. It w̲a̲s̲ dark. It w̲a̲s̲
> snowing. I w̲a̲s̲ walking along a street. There
> w̲a̲s̲ nobody else in the town. I c̲o̲u̲l̲d̲ see a
> light in a window. I c̲o̲u̲l̲d̲ hear someone
> shouting, 'You'r̲e̲ too late! We w̲e̲r̲e̲ here, all
> the time. We w̲e̲r̲e̲ waiting for you, but now
> it'ₛ̲ too late!' Then I woke up. It w̲a̲s̲ a dream!

 Listen again and repeat.

40.2 Listen and mark the underlined words *w* (weak) or *s* (strong).

A: I'ᵐ̲ better than you!
B: No, you aren't!
A: I a̲m̲. I've got more toys than you!
B: No, you haven't!
A: Yes, I h̲a̲v̲e̲! And I c̲a̲n̲ speak twenty languages!
B: You can't! Nobody c̲a̲n̲ speak twenty languages!
A: I c̲a̲n̲. And I c̲o̲u̲l̲d̲ walk when I w̲a̲s̲ three weeks old!
B: You couldn't! That's impossible!
A: I c̲o̲u̲l̲d̲! You don't know – you weren't there!
B: I w̲a̲s̲! I'm older than you!
A: No, you aren't!
B: Yes, I a̲m̲! I'm̲ eight. How old a̲r̲e̲ you?
A: I'm eight hundred.
B: What d̲o̲ you mean? Nobody c̲a̲n̲ be eight hundred years old!
A: Don't argue!
B: I'm̲ not arguing!
A: Yes, you a̲r̲e̲!

Check with the Key. Then listen again and repeat.

40.3 Mark the underlined words *w* if you think they will be weak and *s* if you think they will be strong.

1 I c̲o̲u̲l̲d̲ speak English when I w̲a̲s̲ twelve.
2 I wasn't very well yesterday, but I a̲m̲ today.
3 A: A̲r̲e̲ these your gloves? B: Yes, they a̲r̲e̲. Thanks!
4 A: I don't think you w̲e̲r̲e̲ at the lesson last week, w̲e̲r̲e̲ you? B: I w̲a̲s̲!
5 A: I didn't think the singers in the band w̲e̲r̲e̲ very good. B: Oh, I thought they w̲e̲r̲e̲!
6 A: H̲a̲v̲e̲ you got a pen? B: Just a minute, I think I h̲a̲v̲e̲, somewhere.
7 A: H̲a̲s̲ the lesson started? B: Yes, it h̲a̲s̲, but you can go in.
8 A: Where d̲o̲e̲s̲ he live? B: Near the old town hall. D̲o̲ you know where that is? A: Yes, I d̲o̲.

 Listen and check your answers. Check with the Key. Then listen again and repeat.

41 They're here!
Contractions

A (C69) Listen and look at the spellings of the weak forms (see Units 37–40).

These weak forms written with an apostrophe ,
are called contractions.

full / strong form	contraction / weak form
is	's
is not	isn't

Contractions show the way we normally speak. In the sentence *It's raining again!*, the most important word is *raining*; the word *is* is unstressed and we use the contraction *it's*. But in the sentence *Yes, it is!*, the word *is* is the most important word, and we use the full form, not the contraction.

B (C70) Listen and look at the spellings of the weak forms.

full / strong form	contraction / weak form
are	're

In the sentence *They're here!*, the most important word is *here*, and *They're* is unstressed and contracted to /ðeə/ or /ðə/. But in the sentence *They are*, the most important word is *are*, so we use the full form, not the contraction.

 Note: We use the contraction 's for **is** or **has**.
It's raining. 's = is
Where's he gone? 's = has

Here are some other common contractions.

full / strong form	contraction / weak form
cannot	can't
have	've
had / would	'd

full / strong form	contraction / weak form
I am	I'm
let us	let's
will	'll

We use these contractions in many types of informal writing, as well as in speech.

(C71)

Important for listening and reading

In some types of texts, like cartoons and pop songs, you can find other contractions, like these. Listen.

1 One of these days I'm gonna leave this town.
2 I just wanna have a good time.
3 Nice place, this, innit?
4 A: Why dontcha wanna come with us? B: 'Cos I hate shopping!
5 Rock 'n' roll will never die.
6 Tell 'im to come now!
7 A: Can you see 'em? B: Not yet.

going to	**gonna**	and	**'n'**
want to	**wanna**	them	**'em**
isn't it?	**innit**	him	**'im**
don't you?	**dontcha**	do you	**d'you**
because	**'cos**		

Exercises

41.1 Listen and <u>underline</u> what you hear – the contraction or the full form.

1 A: Why haven't you done the shopping?
   B: *I've / I have* done the shopping. *It's / It is* on the kitchen table.
2 A: The *weather's / weather is* better than last year, isn't it?
   B: It certainly *'s / is*.
3 A: Right then, *I'm / I am* going. Are you coming with us?
   B: No, *I'll / I will* see you later.
4 A: *What's / What is* the time?
   B: *It's / It is* twenty to seven.
5 A: They aren't ready yet.
   B: *We're / We are* ready!
6 A: *I'd / I would* love to go somewhere warm for a change.
   B: *I'd / I would*, too!
7 A: *I'm / I am* afraid they *haven't / have not* arrived yet.
   B: *They've / They have*. *They're / They are* here now!
8 A: *Let's / Let us* go.
   B: I don't think the *concert's / concert has* finished yet, has it?
   A: *It's / It has*, actually.

Check with the Key. Then listen and repeat.

3

5   We are ready.

8

41.2 Listen, and write the sentences you hear in normal spelling.

EXAMPLE
You hear: 'Are you gonna be with us at the weekend?' and you write: 'Are you going to be with us at the weekend?'

1 ....
2 ....
3 ....
4 ....
5 ....

Check with the Key.

42 It's George's birthday
Pronouncing -s endings

We use -s (or -es) endings in four different ways.

- in plural nouns: Why have you got three **phones** on your desk?
- in verbs: She **phones** him every day.
- in possessives: Have you got **Maria's** phone number?
- in the contractions of *is* and *has*: The **phone's** ringing. The **film's** started.

 When we add an -s (or -es) ending to a word, the number of syllables in the word sometimes stays the same. Listen.

day   I'm staying for a **day**.   (1 syllable)
days   I'm staying for two **days**.   (1 syllable)

 But sometimes we add an extra syllable to the pronunciation. Listen.

match   Have you got a **match**?   (1 syllable)
matches Have you got any **matches**? (2 syllables)

Listen and notice the number of syllables in the words on the left.

	number of syllables	
go	1	It's time to go.
goes	1	Hit the ball and watch where it goes.
finish	2	When does the course finish?
finishes	3	Do you know when the course finishes?
George	1	Have you met George?
George's	2	It's George's birthday.
train	1	We're waiting for the train.
train's	1	The train's late again.
box	1	Open the box.
boxes	2	Open the boxes.
boss	1	That's the boss.
boss's	2	That's the boss's office.
glove	1	Is this your glove?
gloves	1	Are these your gloves?
page	1	Which is the right page?
pages	2	This book's got 120 pages.

The rule is that we add an extra syllable if the last sound in the word is one of these:

/s/ /z/ /ʃ/ /ʒ/ /tʃ/ /dʒ/

If the last sound is a vowel, or any other consonant, the number of syllables stays the same.

⚠ **Note:** We don't contract *is* or *has* after /s/ /z/ /ʃ/ /ʒ/ /tʃ/ /dʒ/. Listen.

The food's good. The service is good.
The game's started. The match has started.

Exercises

42.1 Complete these sentences with the correct forms of the verbs and nouns.

1 Let's see who ....._finishes_..... (finish) these .... (exercise) first.
2 The bar .... (close) when the last customer .... (leave).
3 Don't make .... (promise) you can't keep.
4 Nobody .... (use) a typewriter nowadays, do they?
5 My dad's so tall that when he .... (reach) his hand up he .... (touch) the ceiling.

(C76) Listen to check your answers. Check with the Key. Then listen again and repeat.

42.2 Look at the family tree and complete the sentences.

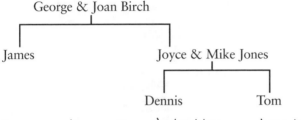

George & Joan Birch

James

Joyce & Mike Jones

Dennis

Tom

EXAMPLE Joyce ...._is_.......... George_'s daughter_ . → _Joyce is George's daughter._
1 Joyce and Mike .... Dennis ....
2 Tom .... Dennis ....
3 James and Joyce .... Mr and Mrs Birch ....
4 Dennis .... George ....
5 Joyce .... Mike Jones ....

(C77) Listen to check your answers. Check with the Key. Then listen again and repeat.

42.3 Look at the picture and answer the questions below.

		Now complete the sentences.
EXAMPLE Whose is the hat?	......_Joyce's_.....	**EXAMPLE** The hat_'s Joyce's_......
1 Whose is the camera?	....	7 The camera ....
2 Whose are the skis?	....	8 The jacket ....
3 Whose is the map?	....	9 The shoes ....
4 Whose is the jacket?	....	10 The skis ....
5 Whose are the shoes?	....	11 The suitcase ....
6 Whose is the suitcase?	....	12 The map ....

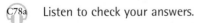(C78a) Listen to check your answers.

(C78b) Listen to check your answers. Check with the Key. Then listen and repeat.

I looked everywhere
Pronouncing past tenses

A

To make the past tense of a regular verb, you add the ending *-ed*:

look → looked   explain → explained

or just *-d* if there is already a letter **e** at the end of the infinitive:

live → lived

Normally, the number of syllables stays the same.

look	(1 syllable)	looked	(1 syllable)
explain	(2 syllables)	explained	(2 syllables)
live	(1 syllable)	lived	(1 syllable)

 Listen.

Look at this!
I looked everywhere.
Can you explain this for me, please?
I explained it but they didn't understand.
Where do you live?
We lived in the country.

NO PARKING

Can you explain this for me, please?

If it's difficult for you to say the *-ed* ending without adding an extra syllable, you can imagine the *-ed* is at the start of the next word. For example, say *I looked everywhere* like this:

I look teverywhere
and say *I explained it* like this:
I explain dit

B

But if the infinitive of the verb ends with /d/ or /t/, the *-ed* or *-d* ending adds an extra syllable:

wait → waited
hate → hated

wait	(1 syllable)	waited	(2 syllables)
hate	(1 syllable)	hated	(2 syllables)

 Listen.

Wait here, please.
We waited half an hour.
I hate waiting.
I hated school.

Important for listening

Sometimes you don't hear the *-ed* ending clearly. This happens when the next word starts with a consonant. Listen.

I look(ed) there.
We liv(ed) near the park.

Exercises

43.1
C82
Listen and mark the verbs with a tick (✔) if you can hear the *-ed* ending clearly, and a cross (✗) if you can't.

1 I watched an interesting film. ✓
2 I watched the news. ☐
3 I walked to the end of the road. ☐
4 The car stopped in the middle of the road. ☐
5 I phoned the police. ☐
6 They helped me a lot. ☐
7 They asked a lot of questions. ☐
8 It rained all day. ☐

Check with the Key. Then listen again and repeat.

43.2
C83
Listen and circle the word you hear.

1 They *play* / *played* very well.
2 We *clean* / *cleaned* all the rooms.
3 We always *cook* / *cooked* a big meal for the whole family.
4 I *need* / *needed* some help with the housework.
5 I *listen* / *listened* to the radio.
6 I *want* / *wanted* to have a word with you.
7 They *arrive* / *arrived* early in the morning.
8 I never *miss* / *missed* the lesson.

Check with the Key. Then listen again and repeat.

43.3
C84
Listen and complete these sentences with the verb form you hear – present or past.

1 We usually ......*finished*...... before the others.
2 You .... my name wrong.
3 I .... a bit of onion to the recipe.
4 I .... those people but they always .... too long.
5 I .... the music in the film.
6 We .... for hours and hours.
7 I .... your house on my way to work.
8 They .... by the sea.

Check with the Key. Then listen again and repeat.

43.4
C85
Listen to this poem.

I wanted to go to the Friday night show.
It started at eight – didn't want to be late.
I walked into town, found the place and sat down.
First in the queue, and nothing to do.
I waited for hours. It rained – a few showers.
A friend passed and asked me, 'Why are you here?
Come down to the pub and we'll have a few beers.'
I remembered just then that Thursday was when
he went for a drink, and I started to think …
Thursday?

Listen again and repeat. Speak with the same rhythm as the recording.

44 Not half past two, half past three
Intonation for old and new information

A 🎧 (D2a) We often use different intonation for old information and new information. Sometimes we repeat the old information with the same words but different intonation. Listen.

A: What time are we meeting? Did you say half past two?

B: No, not half past two, half past three.

(*Two* is old information; *three* is new information.)

A: Edinburgh's one of my favourite places in England.

B: But Edinburgh isn't in England, it's in Scotland!

(*Edinburgh* and *England* are old information; *Scotland* is new information.)

B 🎧 (D2b) Sometimes we only say the old information. Listen.

A: Edinburgh's one of my favourite places in England.

B: But Edinburgh isn't in England!

C 🎧 (D2c) Sometimes we say the old information in different words. Listen.

A: Look – that wine costs £100!

B: Yes, it's expensive, but everything in this shop's expensive!

(*Expensive* is the same information as *costs £100*.)

D 🎧 (D2d) Sometimes we only talk about part of the old information. Listen.

A: I thought that film was really good.

B: Well, I thought the music was good.

(The *music* is part of the *film*.)

Exercises

44.1 Listen and mark the intonation of the words in **bold**.

1 A: How about meeting on Tuesday or Thursday at one o'clock?
   B: I can come on **Tuesday,** but not before **two** o'clock.
2 A: Let's go to the beach and have a swim.
   B: Well, I'll come to the **beach** with you, but I'll probably just do some **sunbathing.**
3 A: Which shop are you talking about? Is it on the corner?
   B: Well, it isn't on the **corner,** exactly, but it's very **near** there.
4 A: When I was at school I was good at maths and physics.
   B: I was good at **maths,** but my best subject was **music.**

Check with the Key. Then listen again and repeat.

44.2 Listen and mark the intonation of the words in **bold**.

1 A: Maybe we could have dinner on Thursday or Friday?
   B: Well, I'm free on **Thursday.**
2 A: Let's have a quick drink at the pub and then go somewhere to eat.
   B: Well, I've got time to go to the **pub** for half an hour.
3 A: Are the shops open in the evenings and on Sundays?
   B: Well, I know they're open in the **evenings.**
4 A: My favourite school subjects were history and geography.
   B: Really? I liked **geography** …

Check with the Key. Then listen again and repeat.

44.3 Listen and mark the intonation of the words in **bold**.

1 A: It's freezing today!
   B: It's pretty **cold,** yes, but it's good weather for walking, so let's **go!**
2 A: Did you go to university in Europe?
   B: I didn't **study** there, no, I just travelled **around.**
3 A: Did you come on the ferry?
   B: No, I like travelling by **sea,** but it takes too **long.**
4 A: We've got plenty of time – we're leaving at four.
   B: That's the **departure** time, yes, but we have to be there by **three.**

Check with the Key. Then listen again and repeat.

44.4 Listen and mark the intonation of the words in **bold**.

1 A: Are the shops open at the weekend?
   B: I know they're open on **Saturdays.**
2 A: What did you think of the band?
   B: The **singer** was good.
3 A: Have you been sightseeing yet?
   B: We've been to the **castle** – that's all we had **time** for today.
4 A: Can I have something non-alcoholic?
   B: We've got some **orange juice** … or some **mineral water** …

Check with the Key. Then listen again and repeat.

45

And suddenly ...
Intonation in storytelling

A (D7a) In storytelling, we often use the past continuous tense for background information and the past simple for main events, and we often use different intonation patterns with these two tenses. Listen and notice the different intonation in the first and second half of each sentence.

1 I was walking along the street one day, and I saw a wallet on the pavement.

2 I was waiting for the bus yesterday, and I heard an explosion.

3 I was lying in bed last night, and I heard a knock at the door.

4 I was watching the news one night, and I saw myself in the shopping centre.

(D7b) Listen and repeat.

street one day – along the street one day – I was walking along the street one day

bus yesterday – waiting for the bus yesterday – I was waiting for the bus yesterday

bed last night – lying in bed last night – I was lying in bed last night

news one night – watching the news one night – I was watching the news one night

a wallet – a wallet on the pavement – and I saw a wallet on the pavement

plosion – an explosion – and I heard an explosion

the door – a knock at the door – and I heard a knock at the door

myself in the shopping centre – and I saw myself in the shopping centre

(D7c) Listen and speak together with the recording.

1 I was walking along the street one day, and I saw a wallet on the pavement.

2 I was waiting for the bus yesterday, and I heard an explosion.

3 I was lying in bed last night, and I heard a knock at the door.

4 I was watching the news one night, and I saw myself in the shopping centre.

B (D8a) We also often use the ∨ type of intonation with other kinds of background information. Listen and repeat.

on Tuesday, I think

as usual

and suddenly

round about midnight

(D8b) Listen and repeat. Then speak together with the recording.

1 I was walking along the street one day, on Tuesday, I think, and I saw a wallet on the pavement.

2 I was waiting for the bus yesterday, as usual, and suddenly I heard an explosion.

3 I was lying in bed last night, round about midnight, and I heard a knock at the door.

4 I was watching the news one night, and suddenly I saw myself in the shopping centre.

Exercises

45.1 Listen and notice the intonation.

> I was doing my **shopping** one day, as **usual**, and I was walking past the **antique** shop, and I saw a beautiful old **vase** in the window, with red and blue and yellow **flowers** on it. And I stood there **looking** at this vase and thinking I'd really like to **buy** it, and I went **in** and **looked** at it and asked about the **price**, but of course it was much too **expensive**. And I did the rest of my **shopping** and went back **home**. And a few days **later** I walked past the same **shop** and noticed that the vase wasn't **there**, and I thought that was the **end** of it. **Anyway**, a couple of weeks **later** it was my **birthday** and I had a little **party** for a few of my **friends**, and they arrived with a huge **parcel** and said, 'Happy **birthday**! We've got a really special **present** for you!' So I **opened** it and guess **what**, it was the **vase** from the **antique** shop!

45.2 Listen and repeat.

I was doing my **shopping** one day,
as **usual**,
and I was walking past the **antique** shop,
and I saw a beautiful old **vase** in the window,
with red and blue and yellow **flowers** on it.
And I stood there **looking** at this vase
and thinking
I'd really like to **buy** it,
and I went **in**
and **looked** at it
and asked about the **price**,
but of course it was much too **expensive**.
And I did the rest of my **shopping**
and went back **home**.
And a few days **later**
I walked past the same **shop**
and noticed that the vase wasn't **there**,
and I thought that was the **end** of it.
Anyway,
a couple of weeks **later**
it was my **birthday**
and I had a little **party**
for a few of my **friends**,
and they arrived with a huge **parcel** and said,
'Happy **birthday**!
We've got a really special **present** for you!'
So I **opened** it
and guess **what**,
it was the **vase**
from the **antique** shop!

As usual

I'd really like to buy it.

Much too expensive

A few days later

A couple of weeks later

Don't look at Exercises 45.1 or 45.2. Tell the story with the help of the pictures. (It doesn't have to be <u>exactly</u> the same story!)

Happy Birthday!

46

Really? That's amazing!
Being a good listener

A

D11a Listen and repeat these phrases – be careful with the intonation.

you see	Well	suddenly
you know	Anyway	then
as usual		
of course		

D11b Listen and notice the intonation where it is marked in the text. Important new parts of the story often have this intonation: ↘

Less important parts, or things we know about already, often have this intonation: ↗ or ↘↗.

I was walking along the street one day, on Tuesday, I think, and I saw a wallet on the pavement. Well, I picked it up and I thought: I'll take it to the police, and I was in a hurry, you see, so I put it in my bag and forgot about it. And I went to work, as usual, and did the shopping, you know, and went home, and then I remembered the wallet. Anyway, I took it out of my bag and had a look inside, and there was some money, and some cards, and tickets and so on, and a photo, and I looked at the photo and suddenly I thought: I know him! It was an old friend from school, you see, and the last time I saw him was years ago. Well, I looked in the wallet and found his phone number and phoned him, and he was pretty surprised, of course, but he remembered me, and we're going to meet tomorrow.

Listen again and repeat.

B

D12a Listen and repeat these phrases – be careful with the intonation.

Oh?	Sorry?	What did you do?	That's great!
Really?	What did you say?	What happened?	That's amazing!
Was it?	Yes.		That's terrible!
Did you?			

D12b This time, A is telling the story and B is listening. Listen and notice the intonation in B's sentences.

A: I was walking along the street one day, on Tuesday, I think, and I saw a wallet on the pavement.
B: Sorry? What did you say?
A: I saw a wallet on the pavement.
B: Oh? What did you do?
A: Well, I picked it up and I thought: I'll take it to the police, and I was in a hurry, you see, so I put it in my bag and forgot about it. And I went to work, as usual, and did the shopping, you know…
B: Yes?
A: … and went home, and then I remembered the wallet. Anyway, I took it out of my bag and had a look inside, and there was some money, and some cards, and tickets and so on, and a photo, and I looked at the photo and suddenly I thought: I know him!
B: Really?
A: It was an old friend from school, you see, and the last time I saw him was years ago.
B: Was it?
A: Yes. Well, I looked in the wallet and found his phone number and phoned him, and he was pretty surprised, of course, but he remembered me, and we're going to meet tomorrow.
B: That's great!

Listen again and say B's part, together with the recording.

Exercises

46.1 Fill the gaps with the phrases in the box.

> That's **amazing!**   Did you?   What **happened?**   That's **terrible!**   Yes?
> What did you **do?**   Sorry?

1 A: I was lying in bed last night, round about **midnight,** and I heard a knock at the door.
   B: Oh? ....?
   A: Well, I went **downstairs** …
2 A: I was waiting for the bus yesterday, as **usual,** and **suddenly** I heard an **explosion.**
   B: ....?
   A: Yes, and I thought, What's **that!?**
3 A: I was watching the **news** one night, and **suddenly** I saw **myself** in the **shopping** centre.
   B: ....?
   A: I said I saw **myself,** on TV!
   B: ....!
4 A: I left my **wallet** on the bus today!
   B: Oh, no! ....!
5 A: **Today** was awful!
   B: Why? ....?
   A: Well, first the bus was late, then …
6 A: I was walking by the river one day last **week,** down near the **bridge,** you **know?**
   B: ....
   A: And I heard a sort of loud **noise** in the water …

(D13) Listen to check your answers. Check with the Key. Then listen again and repeat.

46.2 Fill the gaps with phrases from B on page 100 opposite.

A: I was lying in bed last night, round about
   midnight, and I heard a knock at the door.
B: Oh? ....?
A: Yes, and I thought, 'That's **unusual.'**
B: ....?
A: Well, I went **downstairs,** and looked through the
   window, and it was **dark,** of **course,** but I could see
   a **bus** in the street, with its **lights** off and no
   passengers, and a **man** standing at my door, with a
   sort of official-looking cap on his head.
B: ....?
A: A **cap,** you **know,** like bus drivers wear.
B: Oh, I see. ....?
A: Well, I opened the **door,** and he said, 'Mr **Johnson?',** and I said, 'Yes?' And he said, 'Here's
   your **wallet.** I finished **work** at **midnight** and I **found** it on my bus.' What do you think about
   that?
B: ....!

(D14) Listen to check your answers. (Different answers are possible. There is one possible version on the
recording and in the Key.) Read B's part together with the recording. Then read A's part together with
the recording.

A (D15) When we speak, we can show which words are especially important by giving them a lot of stress. Listen to these two dialogues, and notice the stress and the intonation on the words in **bold**.

A: How good's your English?
B: Well, I can **speak** English quite well, but I can't **write** it very well.

A: Do you know any foreign languages?
B: Well, I can speak **English**, but that's the **only** foreign language I know.

Repeat the dialogues – copy the stress and intonation of the words in **bold**.

How good's your English?

B (D16) Sometimes we use stress to correct what someone says, or to make it more exact. Listen.

A: Is your house number thirty-two?
B: No, it's the next one, number thirty-**four**.

A: Is your house number thirty-two?
B: No, not **thirty**-two, it's number **forty**-two.

Repeat the dialogues.

Is your house number 32?

Exercises

47.1 Listen to each dialogue twice. The first time you listen, <u>underline</u> the two main stressed words in B's
part. The second time you listen, mark the intonation on the stressed words.

EXAMPLE (first time you listen)   A: Have you got the details of the next meeting?
                    B: I know it's on <u>Monday</u>, but I don't know what <u>time</u>.
 (second time you listen)   A: Have you got the details of the next meeting?
                    B: I know it's on <u>Monday</u>, but I don't know what <u>time</u>.

How was the match?

 1 A: How was the match?
   B: The first half was quite good, but the second half was really good.
 2 A: How was the match?
   B: The first half was quite good, but the second half was terrible.
 3 A: Can I come and discuss this tomorrow?
   B: I won't be here tomorrow, but my colleague will be.
 4 A: Can I come and discuss this tomorrow?
   B: I won't be here tomorrow, but I'll be back on Thursday.
 5 A: Have you seen that film? B: I've seen it, but I can't remember
   much about it.
 6 A: Have you seen that film? B: I haven't seen it, but I'd like to.
 7 A: Are you having trouble? B: I know what this word means, but I don't know how to
   pronounce it.
 8 A: Are you having trouble? B: I know what this word means, but I don't know any of
   the others!
 9 A: What did you think? B: I liked the film, but I didn't really understand it.
10 A: What did you think? B: I liked the film, but the seats were so uncomfortable!
11 A: I'd like to go to Britain to study for a month or two – or maybe even a year!
   B: I'd like to go to Britain for a month, but not for a year.
12 A: I'd like to go to Britain to study for a month or two – or maybe even a year!
   B: I'd like to go to Britain, but I'd rather go to America.

Check your answers with the Key. Then listen again and repeat.

47.2 Listen and <u>underline</u> the stressed word or words in B's part of each dialogue. Then listen again and
mark the intonation on the stressed words.

EXAMPLE A: You're June <u>Smith</u>, aren't you?
      B: No, I'm Jane Smith.
 1 A: What's the answer – three hundred and eighty-five?
   B: No – three hundred and ninety-five.
 2 A: After you. B: No – after you.
 3 A: You went to the disco with Steve last night, didn't you?
   B: I didn't go with him – I met him there.
 4 A: Do you live in London? B: Well, not really in London,
   just outside.
 5 A: You said go over the bridge. B: No, I said go under
   the bridge.
 6 A: Were there really fifty people at your birthday party? B: Well, nearly fifty, I think.
 7 A: What's 'Thank you' in Italian? B: I can't speak Italian.
 8 A: How many times have you been to England? B: I've never been to England.
 9 A: Was the course expensive? B: Well, my school paid for the course, but the travel cost
   quite a lot.
10 A: How much should I bring – fifty pounds? B: You'll need at least fifty.

138 + 257 = 385   138 + 257 = 395

What's the answer?

Check your answers with the Key. Then listen again and repeat.

48

Finished? I've just started!
Important words in conversation 2

A

D19a
D19b If we want to give special emphasis to words, for example if we are very surprised, we
sometimes use a lot of stress, and our voices go especially high. Listen to these two dialogues.

  1 A: When will that report be finished?
     B: I've just started it, so it'll be finished this
        afternoon.
  2 A: Have you finished that report?
     B: Finished?! I've just started it!!

D19c In both dialogues, the word *started* is stressed,
but in the second dialogue it is specially
emphasised. Listen and repeat the sentence *I've
just started it* from both dialogues.

I've just started it.
I've just started it!!

D19d In the second dialogue, the word *finished* is also specially emphasised. Listen and repeat.
Finished?!

D19e Listen to the different intonation on *finished* and *started*, and repeat.
Finished?!   started!!

D19f Now repeat the whole answer from the second dialogue.
Finished?! I've just started it!!

B

D20 Listen to two people arguing. Notice the intonation they use, especially on the words in **bold**.

A: You're late! We said two o'clock!
B: We **didn't** – we said **half** past two!
A: We said **two**! You're **always** late!
B: Last time **you** were late! Remember?
A: Was I?

Listen again and repeat the dialogue.

Exercises

48.1 Listen and <u>underline</u> the specially emphasised words in B's replies. Then listen again and mark the
(D21) intonation on the stressed words.

EXAMPLE A: Is that your car?
            B: That? You must be joking!

1 A: Do you like westerns?
   B: Me? I can't stand westerns!
2 A: It's stopped raining.
   B: Really? I don't believe it!
3 A: Is it the first time you've been here?
   B: The first – and probably the last!
4 A: You know the city pretty well, don't you?
   B: Me? I've never been here before!
5 A: What are twelve elevens?
   B: Don't ask me! I'm hopeless with numbers!
6 A: It's two pounds fifty for a cup of coffee.
   B: Two fifty? That's ridiculous!
7 A: Were the shops busy today?
   B: Busy? They were almost empty!
8 A: Do you like rap music?
   B: Like it? I think it's awful!

Is that your car?

Is it the first time you've been here?

Check with the Key. Then listen again and repeat.

48.2 Listen to the telephone conversation between John Watt and Will Knott.
(D22) *Watt* is pronounced like *what*. *Knott* is pronounced like *not*.
Will is a short form of *William* and is pronounced like the verb *will*.

John Watt: **Hello**. Are you **there**?
Will Knott: **Yes**. Who's **that**?
John Watt: **Watt**.
Will Knott: What's your **name**?
John Watt: **Watt's** my name.
Will Knott: **What**?
John Watt: My name's John **Watt**.
Will Knott: John **what**?
John Watt: **Yes**, that's **right**. Are you **Jones**?
Will Knott: No, I'm **Knott**.
John Watt: Well, tell me your **name**, then.
Will Knott: Will **Knott**.
John Watt: **Why** not?
Will Knott: My name's **Knott**.
John Watt: Not **what**?
Will Knott: Not **Watt**, **Knott**.
John Watt: **What**?!

Listen again and repeat the dialogue, using the same stress and intonation, especially on the words in
bold.

49 No, thanks, I'm just looking
Intonation in phrases and sentences 1

Exercises

Intonation varies a lot. You don't always hear the same intonation in the same phrases. But these exercises will help you to notice and practise some of the most common patterns. You should do Units 44 to 48 before Units 49 and 50.

49.1 Listen, notice the intonation and repeat.

A: Ready?
B: Nearly. Warm?
A: No.
B: Cold?
A: No.
B: Raining?
A: Slightly. Umbrella?
B: Thanks. Hat?
A: Here.
B: Thanks.
A: Ready?
B: Yes. You?
A: Yes.
B: Right.

The next version is longer, but the intonation is the same. Listen and repeat.

A: Are you **ready**?
B: I'm **nearly** ready. Is it **warm**?
A: **No**, not really.
B: Is it **cold**?
A: **No**, not really.
B: Is it **raining**?
A: **Slightly**. Do you want your **umbrella**?
B: Yes, **thanks**. Where's my **hat**?
A: **Here** it is.
B: **Thanks**.
A: Are you **ready**?
B: **Yes**. Are you ready?
A: **Yes**.
B: **Right**.

49.2 Listen and mark the intonation on the **stressed** words ↘, ↗ or ↘↗.

1 A: Can I **help** you?
   B: **No, thanks**, I'm just **looking**.
2 B: I'll take **this, please**.
   A: **Sure**. Anything **else**?
   B: **No, thanks**, that's all.
3 A: That's fifteen **forty** altogether.
   B: **Here** you are.
4 A: Here's your **change**.
   B: Thank **you**.
5 A: **See** you.
   B: **Bye**.

Can I help you?

Check with the Key. Then listen again and repeat.

English Pronunciation in Use (Elementary)

49.3 Listen and mark the intonation on the **stressed** words ⬂ , ⬈ or ⬓.

A: Excuse me.
B: **Yes?**
A: Can you tell me the way to the **station, please?**
B: **Yes,** you just go along this **road,** cross the **bridge** over the **river** and there's a big **park** on your **left,** you **know?** **Well,** you go through the **park** and the **station**'s just on the other **side.**
A: Is it **far?**
B: **No,** not **very** far.
A: **OK,** so I go along this **road,** cross the **bridge** and through the **park** – **right?**
B: That's **right.**
A: Thanks very **much.**
B: You're **welcome. Bye.**
A: **Bye.**

Check with the Key. Then listen again and repeat.

49.4 Listen and mark the intonation on the **stressed** words ⬂ , ⬈ or ⬓.

A: All **right?**
B: **Yes.**
A: Not **nervous?**
B: A **bit.**
A: Don't **worry.** It'll be **fine.**
B: I **hope** so.
A: **Right.** Let's **start.** Are you **ready?**
B: I **think** so.
A: **OK.** The first question **is** … What's your **name?**
B: My **name?** … It's … Jack **Johnson.**
A: That's **right!** Well **done! Difficult?**
B: **Well,** not **too** bad.
A: **Right.** The **second** question is … What's 37,548 × 7,726?
B: **What!**

Check with the Key. Then listen again and repeat.

50 Fine, thanks
Intonation in phrases and sentences 2

Exercises

You should do Units 44 to 48 before Units 49 and 50.

50.1 Listen and repeat.

hi	Hi there!
hello	
are	How are you?
fine	
thanks	Fine, thanks.
you	And you?
bad	Not too bad.
hurry	I'm in a hurry.
see you	
bye	

A: Hi there!
B: Hello! How are you?
A: Fine, thanks. And you?
B: Not too bad. I'm in a hurry.
     See you.
A: Bye.

50.2 Listen to the intonation and put the words and phrases in the box into the correct column.

| it was!   usually   is it?   of course!   maybe   really?   I think so   did you? |
| definitely   sometimes |

it was!	usually
....	....
....	....
....	....
	....

Check with the Key. Then listen and repeat.

Listen to the dialogues and repeat.

1 A: Do you think there's life on Mars? B: Maybe.
2 A: This house is two hundred years old. B: Is it?
3 A: Can I borrow your pen? B: Of course!
4 A: Is it hot here in July? B: Usually.
5 A: That was a good meal, wasn't it? B: It was!
6 A: My great-grandfather was a famous artist. B: Really?
7 A: Is this the way to the beach? B: I think so.
8 A: I found some money this morning. B: Did you?
9 A: Do you think it's going to rain? B: Definitely.
10 A: Do you read books in English? B: Sometimes.

Do you think there's life on Mars?

Now listen and answer, using the same phrases. Different answers are possible.

1 Could you help me, please?
2 Do you go out on Friday nights?
3 Today's the longest day of the year.
4 They show some really good films at that cinema.
5 Are you going to Ireland again this year?
6 Do they speak English in Malta?
7 Can you buy stamps in that shop?
8 That was a long trip, wasn't it?
9 Do you have to speak English at work?
10 I won a prize in the lottery last week.

Could you help me, please?

50.3 Listen to the intonation and put the words and phrases in the box into the correct column.

> ~~That's great!~~   ~~That's strange.~~   That's fantastic!   That's interesting.   That's good news!
> That's kind of you!   That's a good idea.   That's marvellous!

That's great! ↘	That's strange. ↗
....	....
....	....
	....
	....

D29b Check with the Key. Then listen and repeat.

D29c Now listen and answer, using the same phrases. Different answers are possible.

 1 I've passed my exam!
 2 I'm sure I left my glasses here but I can't see them anywhere.
 3 I'll help you carry those bags.
 4 They've got lots of English books at the new megastore.
 5 Let's go for a beer.
 6 Look – it's the middle of the afternoon, and all the lights in the house are on.
 7 Would you like to come and stay for the weekend?
 8 Where's Peggy? She said she was definitely coming.
 9 I'm going to Canada for the summer!
10 This road was built by the Romans.

50.4 Listen and repeat.

D30a

thanks	Fine, thanks.
please	Can I have some more, please?
actually	I like it, actually.
Dave?	Are you there, Dave?
if you like	Have some more, if you like.
in fact	Yes, I can, in fact.
probably	About six o'clock, probably.
I'm afraid	No, I can't, I'm afraid.
I think	About twenty, I think.
usually	Coffee, usually.
when you're ready	We can go, when you're ready.
unfortunately	No, it was cancelled, unfortunately.

D30b Listen and use some of the sentences to answer. Different answers are possible.

 1 How are you?
 2 How many people are coming to the party?
 3 This music's awful, isn't it?
 4 Was the concert good?
 5 This cake's delicious.
 6 What time will you be home?
 7 Do you drink tea or coffee for breakfast?
 8 Can you come a bit earlier next week?
 9 Can you speak Hungarian?
10 How old is she?

Chart of phonemic symbols

You can listen to these words on the recording.

D31a **Short vowels**

ɪ	sw<u>i</u>m b<u>ui</u>lding
e	r<u>e</u>d br<u>ea</u>d fr<u>ie</u>nd <u>a</u>ny s<u>ai</u>d
æ	c<u>a</u>n m<u>a</u>p
ʌ	s<u>o</u>n s<u>u</u>n
ɒ	cl<u>o</u>ck h<u>o</u>t
ʊ	f<u>u</u>ll b<u>oo</u>k
ə	<u>a</u>bout exc<u>e</u>llent lett<u>er</u> doct<u>or</u> sug<u>ar</u> Sat<u>ur</u>day
i	happ<u>y</u>

D31b **Long vowels**

iː	tr<u>ee</u> s<u>ea</u>t f<u>ie</u>ld s<u>e</u>cret k<u>i</u>lo
ɑː	c<u>a</u>n't b<u>ar</u> h<u>al</u>f
ɔː	w<u>a</u>ll t<u>al</u>k s<u>aw</u> d<u>au</u>ghter b<u>ou</u>ght w<u>ar</u>m m<u>ore</u> d<u>oor</u>
uː	t<u>oo</u> gr<u>ou</u>p bl<u>ue</u>
ɜː	b<u>ir</u>d w<u>or</u>k t<u>ur</u>n l<u>ear</u>n v<u>er</u>b

D31c **Diphthongs**

ɪə	r<u>ea</u>l h<u>ear</u> b<u>eer</u> h<u>ere</u>
eə	c<u>are</u> h<u>air</u> w<u>ear</u> wh<u>ere</u>
eɪ	c<u>a</u>me r<u>ai</u>n s<u>ay</u> gr<u>ea</u>t w<u>ei</u>ght
aɪ	t<u>i</u>me dr<u>y</u> h<u>igh</u> b<u>uy</u>
ɔɪ	p<u>oi</u>nt t<u>oy</u>
əʊ	c<u>o</u>ld h<u>o</u>me sl<u>ow</u> b<u>oa</u>t
aʊ	n<u>ow</u> s<u>ou</u>nd

D31d **Consonants**

b	<u>b</u>aby jo<u>b</u>
d	<u>d</u>o rea<u>d</u>ing a<u>dd</u>
f	<u>f</u>oot ca<u>f</u>é o<u>ff</u> <u>ph</u>one
g	<u>g</u>o bi<u>gg</u>er ba<u>g</u>
h	<u>h</u>and <u>wh</u>o
j	<u>y</u>es
k	<u>c</u>old tal<u>k</u>ing bla<u>ck</u>
l	<u>l</u>eave ye<u>ll</u>ow fi<u>ll</u>
m	<u>m</u>ore su<u>mm</u>er co<u>mb</u>
n	<u>n</u>ow di<u>nn</u>er go<u>n</u>e <u>kn</u>ow
p	<u>p</u>en sto<u>pp</u>ing hel<u>p</u>
r	<u>r</u>ed so<u>rr</u>y <u>wr</u>ite
s	<u>s</u>ister gla<u>ss</u> pla<u>c</u>e <u>s</u>cissors
t	<u>t</u>en be<u>tt</u>er eigh<u>t</u> wash<u>ed</u>
v	<u>v</u>iew e<u>v</u>ery fi<u>v</u>e
w	<u>w</u>ell a<u>w</u>ay <u>wh</u>ite
z	<u>z</u>ero ro<u>s</u>es s<u>c</u>i<u>ss</u>ors ja<u>zz</u>
ʃ	<u>sh</u>op wa<u>sh</u>ing ca<u>sh</u> ma<u>ch</u>ine <u>s</u>ure na<u>ti</u>onal
ʒ	televi<u>si</u>on u<u>s</u>ually
tʃ	<u>ch</u>oose whi<u>ch</u> fu<u>t</u>ure
dʒ	<u>j</u>eans lar<u>g</u>er fri<u>dg</u>e
ŋ	thi<u>ng</u> ba<u>n</u>k si<u>ng</u>er
θ	<u>th</u>ank nor<u>th</u>
ð	<u>th</u>en mo<u>th</u>er wi<u>th</u>

English Pronunciation in Use (Elementary)

E2 Guide for speakers of specific languages

If your language is one of these, it would probably be useful for you to do these *Sound pairs* (see Section E3).

Arabic
3, 11, 13, 16, 23, 25, 27, 28, 29, 33, 34, 37

Chinese
1, 4, 7, 9, 10, 11, 13, 15, 23, 26, 27, 28, 29, 30, 31, 33, 36, 37

Dravidian languages e.g. Tamil
1, 4, 7, 11, 12, 13, 17, 23, 24, 26, 27, 28, 31, 34

Dutch
1, 3, 4, 5, 8, 10, 12, 14, 15, 26, 28, 29, 30, 31, 32, 33

Farsi
1, 4, 11, 13, 15, 17, 20, 27, 34

French
1, 4, 7, 9, 10, 12, 15, 16, 23, 26, 27, 28, 29, 30, 31, 33, 37

German
10, 12, 15, 21, 23, 26, 28, 29, 30, 31

Greek
1, 2, 4, 7, 9, 11, 12, 13, 15, 17, 31, 32, 33, 34, 37

Italian
1, 9, 11, 12, 13, 15, 16, 23, 26, 27, 28, 29, 31

Japanese
9, 12, 20, 25, 30, 32, 34, 35, 36

Korean
1, 4, 11, 12, 13, 14, 15, 17, 23, 24, 26, 27, 28, 29, 30, 31, 32, 36

Malay / Indonesian
1, 4, 13, 15, 23, 24, 26, 27, 28, 29, 31, 32, 33

Polish
1, 7, 12, 14, 15, 23, 25, 26, 27, 28, 30, 31, 32, 33, 34, 37

Portuguese
1, 4, 7, 9, 13, 15, 23, 25, 26, 27, 28, 30, 31, 34, 35

Russian
1, 7, 11, 12, 13, 14, 15, 17, 20, 23, 26, 28, 30, 32, 34, 37

Scandinavian languages
1, 6, 10, 15, 27, 30, 31

South Asian languages e.g. Hindi, Urdu, Bengali, Gujarati
8, 12, 15, 16, 18, 23, 24, 26, 27, 28, 32

Spanish
1, 4, 7, 9, 11, 13, 14, 17, 20, 23, 26, 27, 28, 33, 34, 35, 37

Swahili
1, 3, 4, 7, 9, 11, 12, 13, 15, 16, 23, 26, 27, 28, 30, 32, 36, 37

Thai
7, 12, 21, 24, 25, 26, 27, 28, 30, 31, 36

Turkish
2, 4, 12, 15, 21, 23, 26, 27, 34, 35

West African languages
1, 4, 7, 9, 11, 12, 13, 15, 17, 18, 23, 26, 27, 28, 29, 31, 34, 36

E3 Sound pairs

If you have problems with hearing the difference between pairs of sounds, you can find extra listening practice in this section. Listen to the sounds and words on the recording, do the exercises and then check your answers with the Key. Note that the recordings for the *Sound pairs* are on CD E.

Sound pair 1 /iː/ and /ɪ/
Sound pair 2 /iː/ and /ɪə/
Sound pair 3 /ɪ/ and /e/
Sound pair 4 /uː/ and /ʊ/
Sound pair 5 /ʊ/ and /ʌ/
Sound pair 6 /uː/ and /əʊ/
Sound pair 7 /æ/ and /ɑː/
Sound pair 8 /ɑː/ and /ɔː/
Sound pair 9 /æ/ and /ʌ/
Sound pair 10 /ʌ/ and /ɒ/
Sound pair 11 /ɒ/ and /əʊ/
Sound pair 12 /əʊ/ and /ɔː/
Sound pair 13 /ɒ/ and /ɔː/
Sound pair 14 /ɔː/ and /ɜː/
Sound pair 15 /e/ and /æ/
Sound pair 16 /e/ and /eɪ/
Sound pair 17 /e/ and /ɜː/
Sound pair 18 /e/ and /ʌ/
Sound pair 19 /ɜː/ and /æ/
Sound pair 20 /ɜː/ and /ɪə/
Sound pair 21 /eə/ and /eɪ/
Sound pair 22 /aɪ/ and /eɪ/
Sound pair 23 /p/ and /b/
Sound pair 24 /p/ and /f/
Sound pair 25 /t/ and /tʃ/
Sound pair 26 /t/ and /d/
Sound pair 27 /t/ and /θ/
Sound pair 28 /k/ and /g/
Sound pair 29 /f/ and /v/
Sound pair 30 /s/ and /θ/
Sound pair 31 /s/ and /z/
Sound pair 32 /s/ and /ʃ/
Sound pair 33 /ʃ/ and /tʃ/
Sound pair 34 /n/, /ŋ/ and /ŋk/
Sound pair 35 /m/, /n/ and /ŋ/
Sound pair 36 /l/ and /r/
Sound pair 37 /h/ and /–/

Sound pair 1: /iː/ and /ɪ/

For more about these sounds, see Unit 2.

(E2a) Listen to the words in the box.

(E2b) Listen. You will hear two words from the box.
If you hear the same word twice, write S (same).
If you hear two different words, write D (different).

leave – live	feel – fill
field – filled	team – Tim

1 .... 2 .... 3 .... 4 .... 5 .... 6 .... 7 ....

(E2c) Listen. Circle the word you hear.

8 *seat / sit*
9 *wheel / will*
10 *eat / it*
11 *cheap / chip*
12 *litre / litter*

Sound pair 2: /iː/ and /ɪə/

For more about these sounds, see Units 2 and 8.

(E3a) Listen to the words in the box.

(E3b) Listen. You will hear two words from the box.
If you hear the same word twice, write S (same).
If you hear two different words, write D (different).

knee – near	B – beer
D – dear	E – ear

1 .... 2 .... 3 .... 4 .... 5 .... 6 .... 7 ....

(E3c) Listen. Circle the word you hear.

8 *cheese / cheers*
9 *knee / near*
10 *we / we're*
11 *D / dear*
12 *he / here*

Sound pair 3: /ɪ/ and /e/

For more about these sounds, see Units 2 and 6.

(E4a) Listen to the words in the box.

(E4b) Listen. You will hear two words from the box.
If you hear the same word twice, write S (same).
If you hear two different words, write D (different).

sit – set	lift – left
litter – letter	listen – lesson

1 .... 2 .... 3 .... 4 .... 5 .... 6 .... 7 ....

(E4c) Listen. Circle the word you hear.

8 *if / F*
9 *six / sex*
10 *in / N*
11 *fill / fell*
12 *disk / desk*

Sound pair 4: /uː/ and /ʊ/

For more about these sounds, see Unit 3.

(E5a) Listen to the sounds and words in the box.

(E5b) Listen. You will hear two sounds or words from the box.
If you hear the same sound or word twice, write S (same).
If you hear two different sounds or words, write D (different).

/uː/ – /ʊ/	pool – pull
fool – full	Luke – look

1 .... 2 .... 3 .... 4 .... 5 .... 6 .... 7 ....

(E5c) Listen. Circle the sound or word you hear.

8 /uː/ / /ʊ/
9 /uː/ / /ʊ/
10 *pool / pull*
11 *pool / pull*
12 *fool / full*

Sound pair 5: /ʊ/ and /ʌ/

For more about these sounds, see Units 3 and 4.

(E6a) Listen to the sounds and words in the box.

(E6b) Listen. You will hear two words from the box.
If you hear the same sound or word twice, write S (same).
If you hear two different sounds or words, write D (different).

/ʊ/ – /ʌ/	look – luck
	book – buck

1 .... 2 .... 3 .... 4 .... 5 .... 6 .... 7 ....

(E6c) Listen. Circle the sound or word you hear.

8 /ʊ/ / /ʌ/
9 /ʊ/ / /ʌ/
10 *look / luck*
11 *look / luck*
12 *book / buck*

Sound pair 6: /uː/ and /əʊ/

For more about these sounds, see Units 3 and 10.

(E7a) Listen to the words in the box.

(E7b) Listen. You will hear two words from the box.
If you hear the same word twice, write S (same).
If you hear two different words, write D (different).

boot – boat	soup – soap
shoe – show	through – throw

1 .... 2 .... 3 .... 4 .... 5 .... 6 .... 7 ....

(E7c) Listen. Circle the word you hear.

8 *too / toe*
9 *grew / grow*
10 *blue / blow*
11 *boots / boats*
12 *shoes / shows*

Sound pair 7: /æ/ and /ɑː/

For more about these sounds, see Units 4 and 6.

E8a Listen to the words in the box.

E8b Listen. You will hear two words from the box.
If you hear the same word twice, write S (same).
If you hear two different words, write D (different).

had – hard	match – March
pack – park	hat – heart

1 .... 2 .... 3 .... 4 .... 5 .... 6 .... 7 ....

E8c Listen. Circle the word you hear.

8 *hat / heart*
9 *match / March*
10 *pack / park*
11 *had / hard*
12 *had / hard*

Sound pair 8: /ɑː/ and /ɔː/

For more about these sounds, see Units 4 and 5.

E9a Listen to the words in the box.

E9b Listen. You will hear two words from the box.
If you hear the same word twice, write S (same).
If you hear two different words, write D (different).

far – four	are – or
farm – form	star – store

1 .... 2 .... 3 .... 4 .... 5 .... 6 .... 7 ....

E9c Listen. Circle the word you hear.

8 *far / four*
9 *R / or*
10 *R / or*
11 *part / port*
12 *star / store*

Sound pair 9: /æ/ and /ʌ/

For more about these sounds, see Units 4 and 6.

E10a Listen to the words in the box.

E10b Listen. You will hear two words from the box.
If you hear the same word twice, write S (same).
If you hear two different words, write D (different).

cat – cut	cap – cup
match – much	ran – run

1 .... 2 .... 3 .... 4 .... 5 .... 6 .... 7 ....

E10c Listen. Circle the word you hear.

8 *match / much*
9 *match / much*
10 *ran / run*
11 *sang / sung*
12 *rang / rung*

Sound pair 10: /ʌ/ and /ɒ/

For more about these sounds, see Units 4 and 5.

E11a Listen to the words in the box.

E11b Listen. You will hear two words from the box.
If you hear the same word twice, write S (same).
If you hear two different words, write D (different).

| luck – lock | nut – not |
| gun – gone | shut – shot |

1 ....   2 ....   3 ....   4 ....   5 ....   6 ....   7 ....

E11c Listen. Circle the word you hear.

8 *lock / luck*
9 *box / bucks*
10 *wrong / rung*
11 *boss / bus*
12 *song / sung*

Sound pair 11: /ɒ/ and /əʊ/

For more about these sounds, see Units 5 and 10.

E12a Listen to the sounds and words in the box.

E12b Listen. You will hear two words from the box.
If you hear the same sound or word twice, write S (same).
If you hear two different sounds or words, write D (different).

| /ɒ/ – /əʊ/ | not – note |
| cost – coast | want – won't |

1 ....   2 ....   3 ....   4 ....   5 ....

E12c Listen. Circle the word you hear.

6 *not / note*
7 *cost / coast*
8 *want / won't*

Sound pair 12: /əʊ/ and /ɔː/

For more about these sounds, see Units 5 and 10.

E13a Listen to the words in the box.

E13b Listen. You will hear two words from the box.
If you hear the same word twice, write S (same).
If you hear two different words, write D (different).

| oh – or | coat – caught |
| woke – walk | so – saw |

1 ....   2 ....   3 ....   4 ....   5 ....   6 ....   7 ....

E13c Listen. Circle the word you hear.

8 *oh / or*
9 *bowl / ball*
10 *coat / caught*
11 *boat / bought*
12 *cold / called*

Sound pair 13: /ɒ/ and /ɔː/

For more about these sounds, see Unit 5.

E14a Listen to the sounds and words in the box.

E14b Listen. You will hear two words from the box.
If you hear the same sound or word twice, write S (same).
If you hear two different sounds or words, write D (different).

/ɒ/ – /ɔː/	shot – short
pot – port	spot – sport

1 .... 2 .... 3 .... 4 .... 5 ....

E14c Listen. Circle the word you hear.

6 *shot / short*
7 *pot / port*
8 *spot / sport*

Sound pair 14: /ɔː/ and /ɜː/

For more about these sounds, see Units 5 and 7.

E15a Listen to the words in the box.

E15b Listen. You will hear two words from the box.
If you hear the same word twice, write S (same).
If you hear two different words, write D (different).

walk – work	saw – sir
born – burn	short – shirt

1 .... 2 .... 3 .... 4 .... 5 .... 6 .... 7 ....

E15c Listen. Circle the word you hear.

8 *walk / work*
9 *born / burn*
10 *short / shirt*
11 *board / bird*
12 *walked / worked*

Sound pair 15: /e/ and /æ/

For more about these sounds, see Unit 6.

E16a Listen to the words in the box.

E16b Listen. You will hear two words from the box.
If you hear the same word twice, write S (same).
If you hear two different words, write D (different).

men – man	head – had
said – sad	pen – pan

1 .... 2 .... 3 .... 4 .... 5 .... 6 .... 7 ....

E16c Listen. Circle the word you hear.

8 *men / man*
9 *said / sad*
10 *met / mat*
11 *set / sat*
12 *bed / bad*

Sound pair 16: /e/ and /eɪ/

For more about these sounds, see Units 6 and 9.

E17a Listen to the words in the box.

E17b Listen. You will hear two words from the box.
If you hear the same word twice, write S (same).
If you hear two different words, write D (different).

get – gate		pepper – paper				
wet – wait		let – late				

1 .... 　2 .... 　3 .... 　4 .... 　5 .... 　6 .... 　7 ....

E17c Listen. Circle the word you hear.

8 *pen / pain*
9 *men / main*
10 *letter / later*
11 *pepper / paper*
12 *edge / age*

Sound pair 17: /e/ and /ɜː/

For more about these sounds, see Units 6 and 7.

E18a Listen to the words in the box.

E18b Listen. You will hear two words from the box.
If you hear the same word twice, write S (same).
If you hear two different words, write D (different).

head – heard	bed – bird
ten – turn	went – weren't

1 .... 　2 .... 　3 .... 　4 .... 　5 .... 　6 .... 　7 ....

E18c Listen. Circle the word you hear.

8 *bed / bird*
9 *ten / turn*
10 *went / weren't*
11 *west / worst*
12 *lend / learned*

Sound pair 18: /e/ and /ʌ/

For more about these sounds, see Units 4 and 6.

E19a Listen to the sounds and words in the box.

E19b Listen. You will hear two words from the box.
If you hear the same sound or word twice, write S (same).
If you hear two different sounds or words, write D (different).

/e/ – /ʌ/	better – butter
when – one	again – a gun

1 .... 　2 .... 　3 .... 　4 .... 　5 ....

E19c Listen. Circle the word you hear.

6 *better – butter*
7 *when – one*
8 *net – nut*

Sound pair 19: /ɜː/ and /æ/

For more about these sounds, see Units 6 and 7.

E20a Listen to the sounds and words in the box.

E20b Listen. You will hear two words from the box.
If you hear the same sound or word twice, write S (same).
If you hear two different sounds or words, write D (different).

/ɜː/ – /æ/	hurt – hat
bird – bad	heard – had

1 ....   2 ....   3 ....   4 ....   5 ....

E20c Listen. Circle the word you hear.

6 *hurt / hat*
7 *bird / bad*
8 *heard / had*

Sound pair 20: /ɜː/ and /ɪə/

For more about these sounds, see Units 7 and 8.

E21a Listen to the sounds and words in the box.

E21b Listen. You will hear two words from the box.
If you hear the same sound or word twice, write S (same).
If you hear two different sounds or words, write D (different).

/ɜː/ – /ɪə/	bird – beard
her – here	were – we're

1 ....   2 ....   3 ....   4 ....   5 ....

E21c Listen. Circle the word you hear.

6 *bird / beard*
7 *her / here*
8 *were / we're*

Sound pair 21: /eə/ and /eɪ/

For more about these sounds, see Units 8 and 9.

E22a Listen to the words in the box.

E22b Listen. You will hear two words from the box.
If you hear the same word twice, write S (same).
If you hear two different words, write D (different).

wear – way	air – A
stair – stay	hair – hey!

1 ....   2 ....   3 ....   4 ....   5 ....   6 ....   7 ....

E22c Listen. Circle the word you hear.

 8 *stair / stay*
 9 *hair / hey!*
10 *there / they*
11 *care / K*
12 *nowhere / no way*

Sound pair 22: /aɪ/ and /eɪ/

For more about these sounds, see Unit 9.

E23a Listen to the words in the box.

E23b Listen. You will hear two words from the box.
If you hear the same word twice, write S (same).
If you hear two different words, write D (different).

my – May	why – way				
die – day	I – A				

1 .... 2 .... 3 .... 4 .... 5 .... 6 .... 7 ....

E23c Listen. Circle the word you hear.

8 *I / A*
9 *white / wait*
10 *like / lake*
11 *buy / bay*
12 *high / hey*!

Sound pair 23: /p/ and /b/

For more about these sounds, see Unit 11.

E24a Listen to the words in the box.

E24b Listen. You will hear two words from the box.
If you hear the same word twice, write S (same).
If you hear two different words, write D (different).

pears – bears	pay – bay
pen – Ben	P – B

1 .... 2 .... 3 .... 4 .... 5 .... 6 .... 7 ....

E24c Listen. Circle the word you hear.

8 *pay / bay*
9 *pen / Ben*
10 *P / B*
11 *pie / buy*
12 *pack / back*

Sound pair 24: /p/ and /f/

For more about these sounds, see Units 11 and 14.

E25a Listen to the words in the box.

E25b Listen. You will hear two words from the box.
If you hear the same word twice, write S (same).
If you hear two different words, write D (different).

pear – fair	pull – full
past – fast	copy – coffee

1 .... 2 .... 3 .... 4 .... 5 .... 6 .... 7 ....

E25c Listen. Circle the word you hear.

8 *pear / fair*
9 *pull / full*
10 *past / fast*
11 *Pete / feet*
12 *copy / coffee*

Sound pair 25: /t/ and /tʃ/

For more about these sounds, see Units 12 and 18.

E26a Listen to the words in the box.

E26b Listen. You will hear two words from the box.
If you hear the same word twice, write S (same).
If you hear two different words, write D (different).

what's – watch	toes – chose
test – chest	coats – coach

1 .... 2 .... 3 .... 4 .... 5 .... 6 .... 7 ....

E26c Listen. Circle the word you hear.

8 *toes / chose*
9 *coat / coach*
10 *beat / beach*
11 *eat / each*
12 *eats / each*

Sound pair 26: /t/ and /d/

For more about these sounds, see Unit 12.

E27a Listen to the words in the box.

E27b Listen. You will hear two words from the box.
If you hear the same word twice, write S (same).
If you hear two different words, write D (different).

try – dry	tie – die
town – down	white – wide

1 .... 2 .... 3 .... 4 .... 5 .... 6 .... 7 ....

E27c Listen. Circle the word you hear.

8 *writing / riding*
9 *two / do*
10 *T / D*
11 *wrote / road*
12 *set / said*

Sound pair 27: /t/ and /θ/

For more about these sounds, see Units 12 and 15.

E28a Listen to the words in the box.

E28b Listen. You will hear two words from the box.
If you hear the same word twice, write S (same).
If you hear two different words, write D (different).

taught – thought	tree – three
boat – both	mats – maths

1 .... 2 .... 3 .... 4 .... 5 .... 6 .... 7 ....

E28c Listen. Circle the word you hear.

8 *taught / thought*
9 *taught / thought*
10 *tree / three*
11 *boat / both*
12 *mats / maths*

Sound pair 28: /k/ and /g/

For more about these sounds, see Unit 13.

E29a Listen to the words in the box.

E29b Listen. You will hear two words from the box.
If you hear the same word twice, write S (same).
If you hear two different words, write D (different).

cold – gold	back – bag	
class – glass	docks – dogs	

1 .... 2 .... 3 .... 4 .... 5 .... 6 .... 7 ....

E29c Listen. Circle the word you hear.

8 *cold / gold*
9 *back / bag*
10 *class / glass*
11 *class / glass*
12 *docks / dogs*

Sound pair 29: /f/ and /v/

For more about these sounds, see Unit 14.

E30a Listen to the words in the box.

E30b Listen. You will hear two words from the box.
If you hear the same word twice, write S (same).
If you hear two different words, write D (different).

few – view	leaf – leave	
ferry – very	lift – lived	

1 .... 2 .... 3 .... 4 .... 5 .... 6 .... 7 ....

E30c Listen. Circle the word you hear.

8 *few / view*
9 *leaf / leave*
10 *ferry / very*
11 *safe / save*
12 *lift / lived*

Sound pair 30: /s/ and /θ/

For more about these sounds, see Units 15 and 16.

E31a Listen to the words in the box.

E31b Listen. You will hear two words from the box.
If you hear the same word twice, write S (same).

If you hear two different words, write D (different).

sing – thing	sort – thought	
sick – thick	mouse – mouth	

1 .... 2 .... 3 .... 4 .... 5 .... 6 .... 7 ....

E31c Listen. Circle the word you hear.

8 *sing / thing*
9 *sort / thought*
10 *sick / thick*
11 *some / thumb*
12 *mouse / mouth*

Sound pair 31: /s/ and /z/

For more about these sounds, see Unit 16.

E32a Listen to the words in the box.

E32b Listen. You will hear two words from the box.
If you hear the same word twice, write S (same).
If you hear two different words, write D (different).

place – plays	Sue – zoo
ice – eyes	rice – rise

1 .... 2 .... 3 .... 4 .... 5 .... 6 .... 7 ....

E32c Listen. Circle the word you hear.

  8 *place / plays*
  9 *Sue / zoo*
 10 *niece / knees*
 11 *piece / peas*
 12 *ice / eyes*

Sound pair 32: /s/ and /ʃ/

For more about these sounds, see Units 16 and 17.

E33a Listen to the words in the box.

E33b Listen. You will hear two words from the box.
If you hear the same word twice, write S (same).
If you hear two different words, write D (different).

so – show	seat – sheet
sort – short	Sue – shoe

1 .... 2 .... 3 .... 4 .... 5 .... 6 .... 7 ....

E33c Listen. Circle the word you hear.

  8 *so / show*
  9 *seat / sheet*
 10 *suit / shoot*
 11 *save / shave*
 12 *sign / shine*

Sound pair 33: /ʃ/ and /tʃ/

For more about these sounds, see Units 17 and 18.

E34a Listen to the words in the box.

E34b Listen. You will hear two words from the box.
If you hear the same word twice, write S (same).
If you hear two different words, write D (different).

shoes – choose	ship – chip
cash – catch	wash – watch

1 .... 2 .... 3 .... 4 .... 5 .... 6 .... 7 ....

E34c Listen. Circle the word you hear.

  8 *shoes / choose*
  9 *share / chair*
 10 *sheep / cheap*
 11 *cash / catch*
 12 *wash / watch*

Sound pair 34: /n/, /ŋ/ and /ŋk/

For more about these sounds, see Unit 19.

E35a Listen to the words in the box.

E35b Listen. You will hear two words from the box.
If you hear the same word twice, write S (same).
If you hear two different words, write D (different).

ran – rang	thin – thing
thing – think	sing – sink

1 .... 2 .... 3 .... 4 .... 5 .... 6 .... 7 ....

E35c Listen. Circle the word you hear.

8 *ran / rang*
9 *thin / thing*
10 *thing / think*
11 *sing / sink*
12 *sun / sung*

Sound pair 35: /m/, /n/ and /ŋ/

For more about these sounds, see Unit 19.

E36a Listen to the words in the box.

E36b Listen. You will hear two words from the box.
If you hear the same word twice, write S (same).
If you hear two different words, write D (different).

might – night	me – knee
some – sun	some – sung

1 .... 2 .... 3 .... 4 .... 5 .... 6 .... 7 ....

E36c Listen. Circle the word you hear.

8 *might / night*
9 *mice / nice*
10 *mine / nine*
11 *some / sung*
12 *swim / swing*

Sound pair 36: /l/ and /r/

For more about these sounds, see Unit 21.

E37a Listen to the words in the box.

E37b Listen. You will hear two words from the box.
If you hear the same word twice, write S (same).
If you hear two different words, write D (different).

light – right	long – wrong
collect – correct	leader – reader

1 .... 2 .... 3 .... 4 .... 5 .... 6 .... 7 ....

E37c Listen. Circle the word you hear.

8 *light / right*
9 *long / wrong*
10 *lock / rock*
11 *collect / correct*
12 *alive / arrive*

Sound pair 37: /h/ and /–/

For more about this sound, see Unit 20.

E38a Listen to the words in the box.

E38b Listen. You will hear two words from the box.
If you hear the same word twice, write S (same).
If you hear two different words, write D (different).

hey! – A	hear – ear
high – eye	hair – air

1 ....   2 ....   3 ....   4 ....   5 ....   6 ....   7 ....

E38c Listen. Circle the word you hear.

8 *hey! / A*
9 *heating / eating*
10 *hold / old*
11 *hate / eight*
12 *heart / art*

E4 From spelling to sound

D32 a–z   These are the commonest pronunciations of letters in words. But there are lots of exceptions, and you will often need to check the pronunciation of words in a dictionary. You can listen to the examples on the recording.

Spelling	Sound	Examples
a	/æ/	bag
a + consonant + e	/eɪ/	late
a	/ə/	about
ai	/eɪ/	train
air	/eə/	hair
ar	/ɑː/	start
ay	/eɪ/	say
au	/ɔː/	taught
aw	/ɔː/	saw
b	/b/	best
c	/k/	car
c + e/i/y	/s/	cent, cinema, cycle
c + consonant + e	/s/	nice
ch	/tʃ/	check
ck	/k/	black
d	/d/	do
e	/e/	end
e	/iː/	me
e + consonant + e	/iː/	these
e	/ə/	happen
e	/ɪ/	England
ea	/iː/	tea
ea	/e/	bread
ea	/eɪ/	great
ear	/ɪə/	hear
ear	/ɜː/	early
ear	/eə/	wear
ee	/iː/	see
eer	/ɪə/	beer
ei	/eɪ/	eight
ey	/eɪ/	grey
ere	/eə/	where
ew	/juː/	new
f	/f/	fly
g	/g/	get
g	/dʒ/	general
gu	/g/	guess
gu	/gw/	language
h	/h/	hat
i	/ɪ/	him
i + consonant + e	/aɪ/	time
ie	/iː/	piece
ie	/aɪ/	pie
ir	/ɜː/	first

Spelling	Sound	Examples
j	/dʒ/	June
k	/k/	key
l	/l/	live
m	/m/	May
n	/n/	no
n + c/k	/ŋ/	uncle, bank
ng	/ŋ/	sing
ng	/ŋg/	single
o	/ɒ/	top
o + consonant + e	/əʊ/	nose
oa	/əʊ/	road
oi	/ɔɪ/	point
oo	/uː/	food
oo	/ʊ/	foot
oor	/ɔː/	door
or	/ɔː/	north
ou	/aʊ/	sound
ou	/uː/	group
ou	/ʊ/	could
ough	/ɔː/	thought
ough	/uː/	through
our	/aʊə/	hour
our	/ɔː/	four
ow	/aʊ/	brown
oy	/ɔɪ/	enjoy
p	/p/	pen
ph	/f/	photo
qu	/kw/	quiet
r	/r/	red
s	/s/	say
s	/z/	easy
sh	/ʃ/	shoe
t	/t/	ten
t	/ʃ/	station
t	/tʃ/	picture
tch	/tʃ/	catch
th	/θ/	three
th	/ð/	father
u	/ʌ/	cup
u	/juː/	music
u	/ʊ/	pull
ue	/uː/	blue
ur	/ɜː/	turn
v	/v/	never
w	/w/	well
wh	/w/	white
x	/ks/	six

Spelling	Sound	Examples
y	/j/	you
y	/aɪ/	try
y + consonant + e	/aɪ/	type
y	/i/	forty
z	/z/	zoo

Silent letters

A lot of English words have silent letters in the spelling – letters which are not pronounced. You can listen to these examples of common words with silent letters on the recording.

Silent letter	Examples
b	climb, comb
d	Wednesday
g	foreign, sign
gh	daughter, eight, high, thought, through
h	hour
k	knee, know
l	could, half, should, walk, would
p	psychology
s	island
t	Christmas, listen, often
w	answer, two, write

E5

The alphabet

Exercises

These exercises will give you practice with the names of the letters of the alphabet.

E5.1 Match the letters with the words that have the same pronunciation.

b	tea
c	pea
i	why
o	bee
p	eye
q	you
r	see
t	are
u	queue
y	oh

Check your answers with the Key.

E5.2 Listen and circle the letter that doesn't rhyme.

(D34) 1 Which letter doesn't rhyme with a?   h   j   k   w
        2 Which letter doesn't rhyme with b?   c   d   e   g   j   p   t   v
        3 Which letter doesn't rhyme with u?   q   w   y

Check your answers with the Key.

E5.3 Listen and write the answers to the questions.

(D35) 1 ....*l*........
        2 ....
        3 ....
        4 ....
        5 ....
        6 ....
        7 ....
        8 ....
        9 ....
       10 ....
       11 ....
       12 ....

Check your answers with the Key.

E5.4
D36
Listen to 12 spellings and write the words. You'll hear the spelling of each word twice – the first time faster, with the letters linked, like this: s‿t‿o‿p, and the second time slowly, like this: s...t...o...p.

Try to write each word the first time, and use the second time to check.

EXAMPLE .... *stop* ....

1 ....
2 ....
3 ....
4 ....
5 ....
6 ....
7 ....
8 ....
9 ....
10 ....
11 ....
12 ....

Check your answers with the Key.

E5.5 Spell these words aloud, first slowly and carefully, and then faster, linking the letters. Remember that we say **gg**, for example, as *double g*.

1 where   2 language   3 who   4 quick   5 called   6 enjoy   7 English   8 only
9 saw   10 getting   11 asleep   12 pronunciation

D37 Listen and check with the recording.

E5.6
D38
Listen to this story and then practise reading it yourself. Notice the pauses between the lines, and the stresses in **bold** (see Unit 33).

> **One day**
> **Leon**ard **Bern**stein,
> the **fam**ous con**duc**tor,
> was re**hear**sing with an **or**chestra.
> **Diff**erent **sec**tions of the **mus**ic
> are **marked** with the letters **A**, **B**, **C**
> and **so** on.
> At **one** moment,
> Bernstein **stopped** the **or**chestra
> and **said**,
> 'F **was**n't very **good**,
> **G** was **bett**er,
> **H** was OK,
> and **I** was fan**tas**tic!'
> The **whole or**chestra started **laugh**ing –
> **Bern**stein **could**n't understand **why**.

E6 Pronouncing numbers

The information and exercises (on page 134) in this section will help you to pronounce different types of numbers.

(D39) 100   1,000   1,000,000

We add *a* /ə/ before *hundred, thousand* and *million*. Listen and repeat.

100	a hundred
1,000	a thousand
1,000,000	a million

Numbers over 100

(D40) When we say numbers over 100, we add the weak form of *and* /ən/ before the last two figures (but not always in American English). Listen and repeat.

101	101 (and)	a hundred and one
350	350 (and)	three hundred and fifty
529	529 (and)	five hundred and twenty-nine
2,491	2,491 (and)	two thousand, four hundred and ninety-one
7,512	7,512 (and)	seven thousand, five hundred and twelve
27,403	27,403 (and)	twenty-seven thousand, four hundred and three

Years

(D41) We say years differently from numbers.
The number 1764 is *one thousand seven hundred and sixty-four*
but the year 1764 is *seventeen sixty-four*.
Listen and repeat.

1764	17/64	seventeen sixty-four
1890	18/90	eighteen ninety
1900	1900	nineteen hundred
1907	19/07	nineteen oh seven

But starting from 2000, we say years the same as numbers.

2000	2000	two thousand
2007	2007 (and)	two thousand and seven

Telephone numbers

(D42a) We say each number separately and pause between groups of numbers. For **0** we say *oh*. Listen and repeat.

01425 365 7098   oh one four two five, three six five, seven oh nine eight

(D42b) For **33** or **77**, for example, we say *double three* or *double seven*, etc. Listen and repeat.

0609 655 400   oh six oh nine, six double five, four double oh

Temperatures

(D43) For **0** we say *zero*. Listen and repeat.

14°	fourteen degrees
0°	zero
−12°	minus twelve (degrees) / twelve (degrees) below zero

Ordinal numbers

 Listen and repeat.

1st	first	20th	twentieth
2nd	second	21st	twenty-first
3rd	third	22nd	twenty-second
4th	fourth	23rd	twenty-third
5th	fifth	24th	twenty-fourth
13th	thirteenth	31st	thirty-first
15th	fifteenth	52nd	fifty-second

Dates

 We can say dates in different ways. Listen and repeat.

22 May	May the **twenty-second**
	the **twenty-second** of May
	May **twenty-second** (American English)
13 January	January the thir**teenth**
	the **thirteenth** of January
	January **thirteenth** (American English)
30 January	January the **thirtieth**
	the **thirtieth** of January
	January **thirtieth** (American English)

Fractions

 Listen and repeat.

$\frac{1}{2}$ a half

$\frac{1}{4}$ a quarter
a fourth (American English)

$\frac{3}{4}$ three quarters
three fourths (American English)

For other fractions, we use the same forms as ordinal numbers.

$\frac{1}{3}$ a third

$\frac{2}{3}$ two thirds

$\frac{1}{8}$ an eighth

$\frac{5}{8}$ five eighths

Decimals

 In decimal numbers, we use the symbol '**.**', and we pronounce it *point*. Listen and repeat.

1.6	one point six
23.95	twenty-three point nine five
0.762	nought point seven six two
	zero point seven six two (American English)

Percentages

 Listen and repeat.

1%	one per cent
50%	fifty per cent
67.3%	sixty-seven point three per cent

Exercises

E6.1 Listen and write the numbers you hear.

D49 1 ....

2 ....

3 ....

4 ....

5 ....

E6.2 Listen and write the numbers of the years.

D50 1 ....

2 ....

3 ....

4 ....

5 ....

E6.3 Listen and write the telephone numbers.

D51 1 ....

2 ....

3 ....

4 ....

5 ....

E6.4 Listen and write the numbers.

D52 1 ....

2 ....

3 ....

4 ....

5 ....

6 ....

7 ....

8 ....

Pronouncing geographical names

Adjectives are often pronounced in a very similar way to the noun; they are not shown separately in the list. For example:

D53a Austria /ˈɒstriə/   Austria /ˈɒstriən/

But sometimes adjectives are pronounced differently; these are shown separately in the list. For example:

D53b Canada /ˈkænədə/   Canadian /kəˈneɪdiən/

D54a
Africa	/ˈæfrɪkə/
America	/əˈmerɪkə/
Argentina	/ɑːdʒənˈtiːnə/
Asia	/ˈeɪʒə/
Atlantic	/ətˈlæntɪk/
Australia	/ɒsˈtreɪliə/
Austria	/ˈɒstriə/

D54b
Belgium	/ˈbeldʒəm/
Brazil	/brəˈzɪl/

D54c
Canada	/ˈkænədə/
Canadian	/kəˈneɪdiən/
Caribbean	/kærɪˈbiːən/
Chile	/ˈtʃɪli/
China	/ˈtʃaɪnə/
Croatia	/krəʊˈeɪʃə/
Cuba	/ˈkjuːbə/
Czech Republic	/ˈtʃek rɪˈpʌblɪk/

D54d
Danish	/ˈdeɪnɪʃ/
Denmark	/ˈdenmɑːk/
Dutch	/dʌtʃ/

D54e
Egypt	/ˈiːdʒɪpt/
England	/ˈɪŋglənd/
Europe	/ˈjʊərəp/
European	/jʊərəˈpiːən/

D54f
France	/frɑːns/
French	/frenʃ/

D54g
Germany	/ˈdʒɜːməni/
Greece	/griːs/
Greek	/griːk/

D54h
Holland	/ˈhɒlənd/
Hungarian	/hʌŋˈgeəriən/
Hungary	/ˈhʌŋgəri/

D54i
India	/ˈɪndiə/
Iran	/ɪˈræn/
Iranian	/ɪˈreɪniən/
Iraq	/ɪˈræk/
Iraqi	/ɪˈræki/
Ireland	/ˈaɪələnd/
Irish	/ˈaɪrɪʃ/
Israel	/ˈɪzreɪəl/
Israeli	/ɪzˈreɪəli/

	Italian	/ɪˈtælɪən/
	Italy	/ˈɪtəli/
D54j	Japan	/dʒəˈpæn/
	Japanese	/dʒæpəˈniːz/
D54k	Korea	/kəˈriːə/
D54l	Mediterranean	/medɪtəˈreɪnɪən/
	Mexico	/ˈmeksɪkəʊ/
D54m	Netherlands	/ˈneðələndz/
	New Zealand	/njuː ˈziːlənd/
	Nigeria	/naɪˈdʒɪərɪə/
	Norway	/ˈnɔːweɪ/
	Norwegian	/nɔːˈwiːdʒən/
D54n	Pacific	/pəˈsɪfɪk/
	Pakistan	/pækɪˈstɑːn/
	Peru	/pəˈruː/
	Poland	/ˈpəʊlənd/
	Portugal	/ˈpɔːtʃəgəl/
D54o	Romania	/ruːˈmeɪnɪə/
	Russia	/ˈrʌʃə/
D54p	Saudi Arabia	/ˈsaʊdi əˈreɪbɪə/
	Scotland	/ˈskɒtlənd/
	Slovakia	/sləˈvækɪə/
	Slovenia	/sləˈviːnɪə/
	Spain	/speɪn/
	Spanish	/ˈspænɪʃ/
	Sweden	/ˈswiːdən/
	Swiss	/swɪs/
	Switzerland	/ˈswɪtsələnd/
D54q	Turkey	/ˈtɜːki/
D54r	Ukraine	/juːˈkreɪn/
	United Kingdom	/juːˈnaɪtɪd ˈkɪŋdəm/
	United States of America	/juːˈnaɪtɪd steɪts əv əˈmerɪkə/
D54s	Wales	/weɪlz/
	Welsh	/welʃ/

E8 Homophones

Homophones are pairs of words with different spellings, and different meanings, but the same pronunciation. For example:

two   /tuː/
too   /tuː/

 Listen. You will hear five pairs of sentences. For each pair, write the two homophones.

EXAMPLE
You hear:
It's two o'clock.   It's too late.
You write:

| *two* | *too* |

1
2
3
4
5
6
7
8
9
10

Check with the Key. Then listen again and repeat the sentences.

Key

1.1

	letters	sounds
1 all	3	2
2 back	4	3
3 could	5	3
4 knee	4	2
5 sixty	5	6
6 thing	5	3
7 who	3	2
8 address	7	5

1.2   1 big   2 dress   3 friend   4 give   5 help   6 next   7 very   8 well

1.3   1 time   2 wash   3 push   4 many

1.4   1 tree   2 shoe   3 what   4 run   5 wait / weight   6 why   7 show   8 near

2.1   1 A: What shall we do this *evening*?
B: Let's stay at home and watch *TV*.
2 A: Let me read that *email*.
B: No – it's a *secret*!
3 A: You know my friend *Steve*?
B: Yes.
A: Well, he's got a new job. He's joined the *police*!

2.2   1 lift   2 minute   3 dictionary   4 window   5 biscuit   6 wings   7 mirror   8 litter

2.3   /iː/ sounds: gr(ee)n m(ee)t p(eo)ple p(i)zza pl(ea)se rep(ea)t t(ea) thr(ee)

/ɪ/ sounds: b(i)g b(u)sy d(i)nner g(i)ve (i)n l(i)sten off(i)ce r(e)peat s(i)x

2.4   1 d   2 e   3 f   4 b   5 a   6 c
1 We're always busy in the office.
2 Would you like tea or coffee?
3 Give me that big green book, please.
4 There were only three people in the museum.
5 Listen and repeat.
6 Let's meet at six o'clock.

2.5   1 leave   2 near   3 letter

3.1   food   June   news   room   school   soup   spoon   Tuesday   two

3.2   1 Do you like fast food?
2 Are you coming to school?
3 It's Tuesday the second of June.
4 Let's watch the news.
5 Room two is over there.
6 Here's a spoon for your soup.

3.3   book   cookery   could   good   looking   sugar

3.4 1 Do you take sugar?

2 Could you help me? I'm looking for a good cookery book.

3.5

/uː/	/ʊ/
true	foot
toothbrush	good
soon	cook
lose	push
through	pull
	put

3.6 1 pool   2 luck   3 soap

4.1 words with /ɑː/: artist   garden   March   part
words with other vowel sounds: square   talk   warm   watch

4.2 words with /ʌ/: country   fun   money   mother
words with other vowel sounds: business   home   lots   push

4.3 1 The butter's too hard.   3 Their son's got dark hair.
2 I'd love to buy that carpet!   4 I first met my husband in Prague.

4.4 1 hat   2 far   3 cut   4 look   5 lock   6 butter

5.1 1 clock   2 gone   3 want   4 wanted   5 sorry   6 what

5.2 1 A: What time is it?
B: I don't know. The clock's stopped.
2 A: What have you got?
B: A box of chocolates.
3 A: Where's the doctor?
B: He's gone on holiday.

5.3 1 thought   2 walked   3 caught   4 taught

5.4 1 bottle   2 salt (and pepper)   3 box (of shopping)   4 floor
5 dog   6 ball   7 door

5.5 This is our kitchen. On the table there's a big *box* full of shopping, a *bottle* of wine and some *salt* and pepper. There's a *ball* on the *floor* and the *dog's* asleep in the corner behind the *door*.

5.6 1 not   2 luck   3 caught   4 short   5 work

6.1 1 hand   2 best   3 egg   4 man   5 men   6 many   7 have   8 next

6.2 7   10   11   12   17   20   70

6.3 1 e   2 f   3 d   4 a   5 b   6 c
1 The first plan was the best.
2 He said 'Thank you.'
3 How many stamps do you need?
4 I haven't got any milk.
5 I'll be back again tomorrow.
6 My friends live in a flat over there.

6.4 1 man   2 cut   3 had   4 paper   5 head   6 set   7 butter

7.1 words with /ɜː/:
1 church   3 dirty   5 nurse   7 shirt   9 third
2 curtains   4 girl   6 purse   8 surfer

words with /ɔː/:
1 door   2 floor   3 four   4 horse   5 shorts   6 warm

words with /ɑː/:
1 car   2 large   3 March   4 parked   5 stars

words with other sounds:
1 beard   2 chair   3 near   4 pair   5 wearing

7.2 1 The *nurse* is sitting on a *chair* next to the *girl*.
2 The boy's *wearing* a *pair* of *shorts* and a *dirty shirt*.
3 There's a man with a *beard* standing *near* the *door*.
4 The girl's *purse* is on the *floor* next to the bed.
5 It's *warm* in the room.
6 The date is the *third* of *March*.
7 There's a picture of a *surfer*, and a picture of *four horses*.
8 There are flowers on the *curtains*.
9 Through the windows, you can see a *church*, with a *large car parked* outside. There are some *stars* in the sky.

7.3 1 34   2 13   3 1st   4 30   5 3rd   6 21st   7 14   8 37

7.4 1 shirts   2 first   3 beard   4 head

8.1 /ɪə/   1 Dear   2 really   3 theatre   4 near
/eə/   1 Mary   2 upstairs   3 there   4 Sarah

8.2 1 She's got *fair hair*.
2 The *chairs* are under the *stairs*.
3 How many *years* have you lived *here*?
4 There's a man with a *beard* sitting in the *square*.
5 Speak up! I can't *hear* you.
6 It's a *clear* day – you can see for miles.

8.3 1 See you next year. /r/
2 We're from England – what about you? no /r/
3 Bye – take care! /r/
4 Bye – take care! no /r/
5 Where shall we meet? no /r/
6 Where shall we meet? /r/

8.5 1 near   2 bird   3 wear

9.1 1 Waiting for the train   3 Raining in Spain   5 Baking a cake
2 Taking a break   4 Making a mistake

9.2 1 write   2 try   3 find   4 buy   5 fly

9.3 1 The plane left in the evening and arrived the next morning. It was a *night flight*.
2 It's best to drink *white wine* with fish.
3 Fourteen kilometres is about *eight miles*.
4 There was no rain yesterday. It was a *dry day*.
5 I think I'm lost – is this the *right way* to the beach?
6 We've had a *great time*, thanks. *Bye!*

9.4 /eɪ/   1 radio   2 table   3 cake   4 train   5 plane   6 suitcase
/aɪ/   7 light   8 wine   9 ice
/ɔɪ/   10 boy   11 coins   12 toys

9.5 1 gate   2 wear   3 my

10.1 1 gone   2 snow   3 lost   4 some

10.2 It's an *old town* on the *coast*. The *houses* are built with *brown stone*. You can get there by train, *coach* or *boat*. In winter there's a lot of *snow* and sometimes the *road over* the *mountains* is *closed*.

10.4 1 coast   2 boot   3 woke

11.1
1 bill	6 pay	11 butter	16 boots
2 piece	7 but	12 part	17 pool
3 buy	8 pack	13 book	18 beard
4 purse	9 bomb	14 party	19 put
5 black	10 pepper	15 back	20 bought

11.2 1 Can you *help* me *paint* the *bedroom wardrobe*?
2 Brian's *blond*, and he's *got* a *big beard*.
3 We're going to the *pub*. It's my *brother's birthday*.
4 Where did I *put* my *black boots*?
5 We asked the waiter to *bring* the *bill*, and it was *double* what we expected!

11.3 1 We'll have to change that *bulb*.
2 Looking for a *job*?
3 It isn't on the *map*.
4 Shall we give him a *tip*?
5 Do we have to walk *up* that hill?
6 *Stop* the bus – I want to get off!
7 I *hope* you have a good time!
8 *Help* yourself!

11.4 1 bears   2 pear   3 copies

12.1 1 2001 was the *first* time I went to Britain.
2 I *found* some money in the street.
3 I worked hard *last* week.
4 Do you know a *good* place to eat near here?
5 I live in *West* Road.
6 Is this the *right* house?
7 Do you want some *bread*?
8 Do you like my new *hat*?

12.2 1 wide   2 wrote   3 set   4 said   5 white   6 send   7 road   8 sent

Key

12.3
1 They *send* us emails every day.
2 I *spent* all my money on CDs.
3 When it stopped snowing we went for a walk across the *wide* fields.
4 People *build* houses next to the beach.

12.5   1 watch   2 wide   3 dry   4 writing   5 taught

13.1
1 give	2 big	3 get	4 comb
5 keys	6 cake	7 kiss	8 ache
9 guest	10 back	11 coffee	12 again
13 walk	14 called	15 bag	16 bigger
17 cold	18 carry	19 work	20 grey

13.2
1 Can I *carry* your *bags*?
2 Give me a *big kiss*.
3 You *gave* me *cold coffee again*.
4 A *grey cat* with *green* eyes *walked* into the *garden*.
5 The *guests* would *like eggs* for *breakfast*.

13.3
1 Shall we *walk*?
2 I came by *bike*.
3 When you go out, *take* the *dog*.
4 I'm going to buy a new *desk* tomorrow.
5 A: You don't *take milk* in your tea, do you? B: I do, in *fact*.
6 It's only seven o'clock and it's already *dark*.
7 Listen and *check*.
8 Mark your answer with a *tick*.

13.4   1 back   2 gold

14.1   1 five   2 visit   3 first   4 free   5 leave   6 photo

14.2
| 1 A fine view | 2 Driving too fast | 3 Knives and forks |
| 4 Five voices | 5 A few vegetables | 6 The lift to the seventh floor |

14.4   1 few   2 leave   3 coffee

15.1   1 month   2 then   3 thin   4 they   5 with   6 birthday

15.2   words with /θ/: thinking   maths   bathroom   things   tooth   teeth   fourth   fifth

words with /ð/: another   the   those   there

15.3
1 The *weather* will be fine for *the* next *three* days. *Then*, on *Thursday*, *there*'ll be some rain in the *north*. The *south* will be dry and sunny, but only about *thirteen* degrees.
2 A: I'm thinking of going to the *theatre* tonight.
   B: Me too! Let's *both* go *together*!
3 A: Are you *thirsty*? B: No, *thanks*.
4 A: *These* are my *mother* and *father*, about *thirty* years ago. And *this* is my older brother – he was about *three* years old.
   B: And *the* baby – is *that* you?   A: Yes, *that's* me, *with* my *thumb* in my *mouth*!

15.4   1 thing   2 tree

16.1   1 say   2 sat   3 leaves   4 east   5 times   6 glasses

16.2 1 Saturday, Sunday
2 Tuesday, Wednesday, Thursday
3 August, September, December

16.3 1 these /z/
2 size /s/ /z/
3 style /s/
4 please /z/
5 isn't /z/
6 pronounce /s/
7 dress /s/
8 it's /s/
9 certainly /s/
10 words /z/
11 suits /s/ /s/

16.4 1 A: Do you like this *dress*? B: The *style suits* you, but *it's* the wrong *size*, *isn't* it?
2 A: Can you *pronounce these words* for me, *please*? B: Yes, *certainly*.

16.6 1 plays 2 zoo 3 so 4 thing

17.1 1 fish 2 station 3 finish 4 shout 5 short 6 dish

17.2 Take your *cash*.
Go to the *shop*.
Buy some *fresh fish* and some *fresh mushrooms*.
Take them home.
Wash them.
Cook them for a *short* time.
Put them in a *dish*.
Eat them.
Shout, '*Delicious*!'

17.3 1 Yes, we're an *international* business. We're based in *Russia*, but we fly to anywhere in *Asia* and the Pacific *Ocean*.
2 A: Why are you *shouting* at that *machine*? B: It's eaten my *cash*!

17.4 1 shoe 2 shoes

18.1 1 watch 2 job 3 chips 4 large 5 juice 6 jazz 7 chair 8 age

18.2 1 get 2 Christmas 3 give 4 picture

18.4 words with /tʃ/: teacher chair chicken cheap Dutch chips cheese
words with /dʒ/: lounge bridge large juice language orange dangerous

18.5 1 orange juice 2 Dutch cheese 3 A cheap chair 4 a language teacher
5 chicken and chips 6 A dangerous bridge 7 a large lounge

18.6 1 watch 2 choose 3 what's 4 coats

19.1 1 moon 2 wrong 3 drink 4 uncle 5 knives 6 comb 7 thing 8 stronger

19.2 words with /n/: knee nose
words with /ŋ/: tongue ring ankle

19.3 1 A warm evening 2 A wrong answer 3 My hungry uncle
4 A single room 5 Nine languages

19.4 1 The woman's *listening* to the radio and *reading*.
2 The phone's *ringing*.
3 The cat's *drinking*.
4 It's *snowing*.

19.5   1 rang   2 think   3 night   4 sung   5 some

20.1   1 hat   2 how   3 home   4 half   5 high / hi   6 who

20.2   A: Excuse me, can you tell me *how* to get to the castle?
B: Yes. Go past the *hotel* and the *hospital*, then there's a road *behind* those *houses*.
You go up a *hill*, and the castle's at the top.
A: Thanks for your *help*!

20.3   1 A helping hand   2 A happy holiday   3 How many hours?   4 History, perhaps?
5 Half a house   6 How did it happen?   7 Hi! Who's at home?

20.4   1 ear   2 high

21.1   1 late   2 light   3 large   4 cold   5 table   6 apple   7 learning   8 below

21.2   1 Did you say the *letter* box or the *litter* bin?
2 *Hello*. My name's L. I'm the twelfth *letter* of the alphabet.
3 There's an *apple* in the *middle* of the *table*.
4 Would you like a *single* room or a *double*?
5 What's in that *little bottle*?

21.3   My bus was *late*.
I *lost* my wallet.
I *fell* off a ladder.
I caught a *cold*.
I *fell asleep* at work.
That's *life*!

21.4   1 light   2 correct

22.1   1 Hey, look! I found these old *rock records* in a *rubbish* bin!
2 *Rain* again – what *terrible* weather!
3 Are you *really* sure this is the *right address*?
4 Stop *running round* the *room*! We've got to get *ready* to go out.
5 A: Oh, no, I've lost an *earring*. B: I'm afraid Anna *borrowed* it.
6 A: *Hurry* up! B: Why? It isn't a *race*. A: We're *already* late! B: Don't *worry*, they'll wait till we *arrive*.

22.2   *Underlining = /r/ pronounced*
1 A: Where did you pa<u>r</u>k the ca<u>r</u>? B: I'm not su<u>r</u>e. I think it was just around the co<u>r</u>ne<u>r</u>.
2 A: Have you ever heard of squa<u>r</u>e oranges? B: No, never!
3 A: Can you play the guitar? B: I can play the guita<u>r</u> and sing.
4 A: A<u>r</u>e we fa<u>r</u> away from the road? B: Well, it's rathe<u>r</u> ha<u>r</u>d to say …

22.3   1 right   2 long   3 correct

23.1   1 news   2 few   3 yet   4 weekend   5 tunes
6 when   7 music   8 west   9 yellow   10 year

23.2   1 A: *When's* your interview?
B: It's on *Wednesday*, at *quarter* past one.
A: Good luck!
2 A: Are you going *away* for the *weekend*?
B: Yes.
A: *Where*?
B: I don't know *yet*.

3 A: Hi! *Where* are you?

  B: We're in *west* Wales.

  A: What's the *weather* like?

  B: *Yesterday* was *wet* and *windy*, but today's beautiful.

4 A: Can you read *music*?

  B: No, but I remember a *few tunes* from when I was *young*.

23.3
What?	A wallet.
What colour?	Yellow.
With?	Money, keys, cards – the usual things.
Where?	In the town square.
When?	Yesterday.
What time?	Twelve.
Who?	Two young men.
What happened?	I was waiting in a queue. They were quick. They ran away.

24.1   1 Tuesday   2 fifty   3 expensive   4 centimetre   5 pencil
       6 December   7 September   8 bedroom   9 October   10 exam

24.2   1 mountains   2 reception   3 accident   4 postcard   5 sunglasses, umbrella

24.3   1 A: How's your E<u>ng</u>lish?

  B: I think I need to pra<u>c</u>tise more – I have pro<u>bl</u>ems with making sen<u>ten</u>ces, and ten<u>s</u>es, and pronun<u>c</u>iation, and li<u>s</u>tening, and a<u>n</u>swering que<u>st</u>ions, and co<u>nv</u>ersation, and I make too many mi<u>st</u>akes …

  A: Don't worry, it's not so bad! You're a<u>lm</u>ost an e<u>xp</u>ert!

2 A: Where's my pa<u>ssp</u>ort?

  B: I don't know. In your sui<u>tc</u>ase, maybe?

  A: Where's my sui<u>tc</u>ase?

  B: U<u>pst</u>airs, in the war<u>dr</u>obe.

  A: Right. And where's the e<u>nv</u>elope that was on the ki<u>tch</u>en table?

  B: In the wa<u>st</u>epaper ba<u>sk</u>et – was it i<u>mp</u>ortant?

25.1   1 Is that your *dress*?

2 Is it going to *rain*?

3 A few *miles*.

4 I went to a *cool* party.

5 Are you *asleep*?

6 Are you going by *train*?

7 Is that your *address*?

8 How did you *sleep*?

9 A few *smiles*.

10 I went to a *school* party.

11 Is he your *twin*?

12 Is he going to *win*?

25.2   *A different order is also possible.*

1 pay, play, plane, plate, rain, train, late, paint, eight

2 see/sea, tea, feet, seat, three, free, tree, street, eat

3 so, low, no/know, slow, soap, slope, nose/knows

4 lie, fight, right, light, flight

25.3   1 plane   2 blue   3 drink   4 twelfth   5 free   6 o'clock   7 speak   8 floor

26.1   1 cold   2 colder   3 dancer   4 dance   5 older
       6 old   7 centre   8 centre   9 fast   10 faster

1 Yesterday was *cold*, but today's *colder*.

2 My wife's a good *dancer* but I can't *dance* at all.

3 I'm *older* than you, but not too *old* to learn English.

4 I *sent* my daughter to buy some things in the shopping *centre*.

5 The bus is *fast* but the train's *faster*.

26.3 1 A: Have you seen that fi<u>lm</u>? B: No, I ha<u>ven't</u>.
2 A: Be there at si<u>x</u>. B: Is that when it star<u>ts</u>?
3 A: Have you been to Fra<u>nce</u>? B: Yes, o<u>nce</u>.
4 A: How do you say 'Hello' in Fre<u>nch</u>? B: I ca<u>n't</u> speak Fre<u>nch</u>?
5 A: Have some of these biscui<u>ts</u>. B: No, tha<u>nks</u>, I do<u>n't</u> like them.
6 A: I fo<u>und</u> some money in the street today. B: How much? A: Fifty pe<u>nce</u>.
7 A: Wha<u>t's</u> for lu<u>nch</u>? B: Fish and chi<u>ps</u>.
8 A: I only sle<u>pt</u> si<u>x</u> hours la<u>st</u> night. B: I di<u>dn't</u> sleep at all!
9 A: What colour are your new glo<u>ves</u>? B: Pi<u>nk</u> and ora<u>nge</u>!

26.4 1 physics   2 isn't   3 thousands   4 boots   5 banks   6 silence   7 west

27.1 1 See you *next* week.
2 Have a *good* time.
3 Have a *great* holiday.
4 *Give* me a call.
5 *Send* me an email.
6 *Tell* me how you are.
7 *Write* me a letter.
8 *Bring* me a present.

27.2 1 I<u>t's</u> really war<u>m</u> today.
2 Try thi<u>s</u> sentence.
3 I do<u>n't</u> know wha<u>t</u> to do.
4 Look <u>th</u>rough a<u>ll</u> the photos.
5 Check <u>th</u>e answer.
6 I<u>'d</u> like <u>t</u>o a<u>sk</u> you something.
7 I<u>s</u> this the right p<u>l</u>ace?
8 I have<u>n't</u> listene<u>d</u> to thi<u>s</u> CD yet.
9 The meeti<u>ng's</u> o<u>n</u> Monday.
10 The potatoes are<u>n't c</u>ooke<u>d</u> yet.

27.3 *A different order is also possible.*

this month	next month	last month
a big town	an old town	a small town
a young cat	a white cat	a big cat
a black cat	an old cat	a small cat
cheap clothes	white clothes	big clothes
black clothes	old clothes	small clothes

28.1 1 eyes 1   6 glass 1
2 why 1   7 glasses 2
3 white 1   8 university 5
4 write 1   9 business 2
5 writing 2   10 information 4

28.2 1 Saturday   2 Two   3 Eleven, seventeen   4 W ('double u')   5 March, May, June

28.3 I remember(3) once on my first visit(2) to England(2), soon after(2) I started(2) learning(2) English(2), my landlady(3) went shopping(2) and she came back with a big bag full of things, but she forgot(2) to buy some soup – she needed(2) a tin of tomato(3) soup. So I said, 'I'll go to the shop and buy it for you,' because(2) I wanted(2) to be helpful(2) and it was a chance to practise(2) my English(2) a bit. So I went to the little(2) shop round the corner(2) and asked the shopkeeper(3) for tomato(3) soup. But he seemed surprised(2), he didn't(2) understand(3), and I repeated(3) again(2) and again(2) 'soup, tomato(3) soup' until(2) he gave me some red soap, and I realised(2) I'd confused(2) 'soup' and 'soap' and I was asking(2) for 'tomato(3) soap'. I felt terrible(3), I wanted(2) to run out of the shop, but my landlady(3) wanted(2) her soup, so I said, 'Thank you. And tomato(3) soup, please' – this time with the correct(2) pronunciation – and he gave me the soup. I paid and went back to the house and said to the landlady(3), pronouncing(3) very(2) carefully(3), 'Here's your soup, and I bought you this soap as a present(2),' and she said, 'Ooh, thank you very much, that's very(2) nice of you!'

29.1

1 Britain	2 today	3 America	4 police
5 another	6 again	7 mountain	

1 Great Britain	2 arriving today	3 going to America	4 call the police
5 have another	6 say it again	7 climb the mountain	

29.2 Where's the <u>waiter</u>? – Can you <u>wait a</u> minute?
Not <u>at all</u>. – You'll see <u>a tall</u> building on your left.
Look in the <u>cellar</u>. – I'm trying to <u>sell a</u> house.
It takes <u>a long</u> time. – Walk <u>along</u> the beach.
Smoking isn't <u>allowed</u>. – I heard <u>a loud</u> noise.
I'd like to live in a <u>newer</u> house. – My father <u>knew a</u> lot about music.

29.3

1 America	2 sentence	3 different	4 mountain
5 today	6 letter	7 police	8 again

30.1 1 afraid 2 better 3 police 4 correct 5 enjoy

30.2 words with first-syllable stress: longer turning sleeping
words with second-syllable stress: asleep along return

30.3 OooOo 1 teacher or student?
2 reading or writing?
OoooO 1 single or return?
2 finish or begin?
oOoOo 1 the same or different?
2 perhaps or maybe?
oOooO 1 asleep or awake?
2 behind or in front?

30.4 1 /'sɪstə/ sister
2 /rɪ'læks/ relax
3 /'piːpl/ people
4 /'fɪnɪʃ/ finish
5 /kəm'pliːt/ complete
6 /'teɪbl/ table
7 /prə'naʊns/ pronounce

31.1

1 interview	2 museum	3 magazine	4 definitely
5 American	6 politician	7 nationality	8 photography

31.2

Ooo	oOo
adjective	eleven
alphabet	important
cinema	reception
furniture	remember
grandmother	tomorrow

31.3
1 We had a *delicious* meal on *Saturday*.
2 We *normally* go on *holiday* by car, but this time we're going by *bicycle*.
3 I did ten grammar *exercises yesterday*.
4 Is *Switzerland* an *expensive* country?
5 My son's *seventeen* and my father's *seventy*.
6 I had a long *telephone conversation* this *afternoon*.

31.4

Oooo	January February
oOo	September October November December

32.1 1 half-price   2 second class   3 mobile phone   4 city centre

32.2 earrings   wine bar   handbag   birthday present   boyfriend
A: Oh no, I can't find my earrings!
B: Have you looked in your handbag?
A: Of course!
B: Maybe you left them in that wine bar last night?
A: Oh no, maybe I did!
B: Are they important?
A: Yes – they were a birthday present from my boyfriend!

Checklist
Have I …
… set the alarm clock?
… and put it on the bedside table?
… put my plane ticket in my trouser pocket?
… packed my toothbrush?
… put my suitcase by the bedroom door?
… switched the CD player off?
… phoned the taxi driver to say 'Be here at six'?
Have I …
Have I …
… Where's my checklist?!

33.1 A few years ago / I read in a newspaper / that the staff at a library / in a small town in the west of England / had noticed / that the number of visitors to the library / was going down and down, / and the number of books they were borrowing / was going down even faster. / They couldn't understand this, / so they decided to do some research / to find out the reason. / They interviewed people / and asked them to fill in questionnaires / and so on. / And guess what they discovered. / The reason was / simply / that everybody had read all the books already!

A few <u>years</u> ago / I read in a <u>newspaper</u> / that the staff at a <u>library</u> / in a small town in the west of <u>England</u> / had <u>noticed</u> / that the number of <u>visitors</u> to the library / was going <u>down</u> and <u>down</u>, / and the number of <u>books</u> they were borrowing / was going down even <u>faster</u>. / They couldn't <u>understand</u> this, / so they decided to do some <u>research</u> / to find out the <u>reason</u>. / They <u>interviewed</u> people / and asked them to fill in <u>questionnaires</u> / and <u>so</u> on. / And guess what they <u>discovered</u>. / The reason <u>was</u> / <u>simply</u> / that everybody had <u>read</u> all the books <u>already</u>!

33.2 This seems unbelievable / but it's a true story / in fact. A farmer / was working in the fields / with his tractor. / The tractor crashed / and he fell out / and landed on the ground / unconscious. / As he fell, / his mobile phone / fell out of his pocket. / Soon after, / a bird that was flying around the fields / saw the phone / and started pecking it / with its beak. / Amazingly / it dialled the number 999 / and soon the emergency services arrived / to help the farmer.

This seems <u>unbelievable</u> / but it's a <u>true</u> <u>story</u> / in <u>fact</u>. A <u>farmer</u> / was working in the <u>fields</u> / with his <u>tractor</u>. / The tractor <u>crashed</u> / and he <u>fell</u> <u>out</u> / and <u>landed</u> on the <u>ground</u> / <u>unconscious</u>. / As he <u>fell</u>, / his <u>mobile</u> <u>phone</u> / <u>fell</u> out of his <u>pocket</u>. / <u>Soon</u> <u>after</u>, / a <u>bird</u> that was flying around the <u>fields</u> / <u>saw</u> the phone / and started <u>pecking</u> it / with its <u>beak</u>. / <u>Amazingly</u> / it dialled the number <u>999</u> / and soon the <u>emergency</u> services arrived / to <u>help</u> the farmer.

34.1
1 Choose the correct answer and tick it.
2 Which page is it on?
3 How do you spell it?
4 How do you pronounce it?
5 What does it mean?
6 I can't understand this.
7 Look it up in your dictionary.
8 It isn't easy to speak English.
9 Listen – which language is that?
10 Don't worry if you make a mistake.

34.2
1 A: What do you think of yoga? B: I don't know, I've never *tried* it.
2 A: What happened to my favourite cup? B: It *fell* off the table.
3 A: Which film shall we go to? B: I don't mind. I've *seen* all of them before.
4 A: You look pleased. B: Yes, I've *found* a new job.
5 A: What did you do last night? B: I just *stayed* at home.
6 A: Where did you buy that hat? B: I *made* it myself!
7 A: Does your dog like biscuits? B: I don't know, I've never *asked* it.
8 A: How did you get here? B: I *swam* across the river.

34.3
1 Where are you going?
2 Where shall we go?
3 Where did I put my scissors?
4 I don't know where I put my scissors.
5 Have another biscuit.
6 Have another apple.
7 They're all coming with us.
8 They're coming with us.
9 Are you sure?
10 Are you sure about that?

35.1
1 A: *Do you* ᵂ*often* go swimming? B: Not really, I ʲonly go ᵂonce or twice a month.
2 A: What's *the* ʲ*eighth* letter in the ʲalphabet? B: Maybe ʲit's G ʲor H *or* I ʲor J?
3 A: When do you *go* ᵂ*on* holiday? B: We ᵘusually go ᵂin July ʲor August.
4 A: What's your *new* ᵂ*address*? B: Twenty ʲeight, Sea ʲAvenue.
5 A: Try *to* ᵂ*answer* soon. B: OK, I'll send you my ʲanswer *by* ʲ*email*.
6 A: Look! There's *snow* ᵂ*on* the mountains. B: Really? I can't *see* ʲ*anything*.

35.2
1 Is it blue ʷor grey?
2 What day ʲis it today? Thursday ʲor Friday?
3 Coffee ʲor tea?
4 Where's my ʲinterview suit?
5 Play ʲa song for me.
6 Hello. Reception? Which city ʲis this?
7 See you ʷin the ʲevening.
8 Why do we ʲalways have to get up so ʷearly?

35.3
1 A: Are you the new ʷassistant? B: Yes, I ʲam.
2 A: Is he ʲin the same class as you? B: No, he ʲisn't.
3 A: Am I late? B: No, you ʷaren't. Come in.
4 A: Is she coming with us? B: Yes, she ʲis.
5 A: These chairs aren't very comfortable, are they? B: No, they ʲaren't.

36.1

1 OoOo
what's the matter?
see you later
tell the others
feeling better
come for dinner
round the corner
go and find it
what's the problem?
one pound forty
half a kilo
sixty-seven
breakfast's ready

2 OooO
what shall we do?
stand in the queue
what about you?
nothing to do
anyone there?
ready to go
on the TV
two and a half
asking for more
now and again
leave it to me
quarter to four

36.2
Pass me the *jam*, Pam
Wait in the queue, Sue
See you *again*, Jen
Leave it to me, Lee
What would you *like*, Mike?
When shall we meet, Pete?
Over the *hill*, Bill
Where have you gone, John?
Soon as you *can*, Van
Almost forgot, Scott
Lend me your *pen*, Ben
Where shall we go, Flo?
Get a new *job*, Bob
How do you feel, Neil?
What have you *got*, Dot?

36.3
Take me to the *show*, Jo
Thank you for the food, Jude
See you in the *park*, Mark
Really like the hat, Pat
See you on the *train*, Jane
When will you be back, Jack?
Always on the *phone*, Joan
When did you arrive, Clive?
Have a glass of *juice*, Bruce.

150   *English Pronunciation in Use (Elementary)*

37.1　1　A: Are you (w) going to talk to him (w)? B: No, I think he (s) should talk to me (s) first.

2　A: Shall I phone her (w)? B: Yes, I (w) think you (w) should.

3　A: You (w) see those people over there? Do you (w) know them (w)? B: I know her (s), but I don't know him (s).

4　A: What are you (w) going to give him (w)? B: I think I'll give him (w) a shirt. What about you (s)?

5　Let him (w) come in and ask him (w) what he (w) wants.

6　She (w) says she'll (w) bring her (w) money tomorrow.

7　I'm tired … shall we (w) go now?

8　Everybody's leaving. What about us (s)? Shall we (s) go, too?

9　Tell us (w) when you're (w) ready.

10　A: Who broke that window? B: He (s) did! C: No, I didn't, she (s) did!

37.2　1　What *do you* think about it?

2　Where *shall we go* tonight?

3　He's ready *for you* now.

4　Where *is he*?

5　*Tell them to* come in.

6　*Are you* feeling all right?

7　Tell *me the news*.

8　*I know her* phone number but not *her address*.

38.1　1　They went out and (w) left their (w) children at (w) home.

2　Don't sit there – that's his (s) seat.

3　Is this the train to (s) London or from (s) London?

4　I didn't say at (s) five o'clock, I said about five o'clock.

5　What are (w) you going to (w) do?

6　His (w) first name's Jack, but I don't know his (w) second name.

7　Would you like some (w) more tea?

8　Bring your (w) umbrella – it's going to (w) rain.

9　Excuse me – is this your (s) umbrella?

10　Can you go and (w) buy some (w) bread and (w) milk, please?

11　You've bought some (w) flowers – who are they for (s)?

12　I bought them (w) for (w) you (s)!

39.1　*On the recording it says:*

There are four people in the car.

There's a woman sitting in the house.

There are some children walking along the road.

There are no clouds in the sky.

There's another house on the right.

39.2　There's a cat on the mat.

There's a fish in a dish.

There's a dog in the fog,

and a mouse in the house.

There's a film on TV.

You can sit on my knee.

There are two cups of tea.

One for you, one for me.

39.3 1 Tessa's taller *than* Terry, but she isn't *as tall as* Ted.

2 Ted's *older than* Tessa, but he isn't *as old as* Terry.

3 A: What's the longest tunnel in the world?

B: The Channel Tunnel, between England and France?

A: No, *there's* a *longer* one *than* that.

B: Is *there*, really?

A: Yes, *there* is, in Japan.

4 A: How many dollars are *there* in a pound?

B: I think *there are* about one and a half … or maybe *there are* one and a half pounds in a dollar?

39.4 A: What <u>are</u>(w) <u>you</u>(w) doing <u>there</u>(s)?

B: <u>There</u>(w)'s <u>a</u>(w) spider in the room.

A: Is <u>there</u>(w)? Where?

B: <u>There</u>(s), look!

A: No, <u>there</u>(w) isn't!

B: Yes, <u>there</u>(w) is!

A: Well, actually, <u>there</u>(w) <u>are</u>(w) two – one <u>there</u>(s) <u>and</u>(w) one <u>there</u>(s)!

40.2 A: I'<u>m</u> (w) better than you!

B: No, you aren't!

A: I <u>am</u> (s). I'<u>ve</u> (w) got more toys than you!

B: No, you haven't!

A: Yes, I <u>have</u> (s)! And I <u>can</u> (w) speak twenty languages!

B: You can't! Nobody <u>can</u> (w) speak twenty languages!

A: I <u>can</u> (s). And I <u>could</u> (w) walk when I <u>was</u> (w) three weeks old!

B: You couldn't! That's impossible!

A: I <u>could</u> (s)! You don't know – you weren't there!

B: I <u>was</u> (s)! I'm older than you!

A: No, you aren't!

B: Yes, I <u>am</u> (s)! I'<u>m</u> (w) eight. How old <u>are</u> (w) you?

A: I'<u>m</u> (w) eight hundred.

B: What <u>do</u> (w) you mean? Nobody <u>can</u> (w) be eight hundred years old!

A: Don't argue!

B: I'<u>m</u> (w) not arguing!

A: Yes, you <u>are</u> (s)!

40.3 1 I <u>could</u> (w) speak English when I <u>was</u> (w) twelve.

2 I wasn't very well yesterday, but I <u>am</u> (s) today.

3 A: <u>Are</u> (w) these your gloves? B: Yes, they <u>are</u> (s). Thanks!

4 A: I don't think you <u>were</u> (w) at the lesson last week, <u>were</u> (s) you? B: I <u>was</u> (s)!

5 A: I didn't think the singers in the band <u>were</u> (w) very good. B: Oh, I thought they <u>were</u> (s)!

6 A: <u>Have</u> (w) you got a pen? B: Just a minute, I think I <u>have</u> (s), somewhere.

7 A: <u>Has</u> (w) the lesson started? B: Yes, it <u>has</u> (s), but you <u>can</u> (w) go in.

8 A: Where <u>does</u> (w) he live? B: Near the old town hall. <u>Do</u> (w) you know where that is? A: Yes, I <u>do</u> (s).

41.1 1 A: Why haven't you done the shopping? B: I *have* done the shopping. *It's* on the kitchen table.

2 A: The *weather's* better than last year, isn't it? B: It certainly *is*.

3 A: Right then, *I'm* going. Are you coming with us? B: No, *I'll* see you later.

4 A: *What's* the time? B: *It's* twenty to seven.

5 A: They aren't ready yet. B: *We are* ready!

6 A: *I'd* love to go somewhere warm for a change. B: I *would*, too!

7 A: *I'm* afraid they *haven't* arrived yet. B: *They have*. *They're* here now!

8 A: *Let's* go. B: I don't think the *concert's* finished yet, has it? A: *It has*, actually.

41.2
1 What do you want to do tomorrow?
2 We'll just have to wait and see.
3 I was late because there was a lot of traffic.
4 Bring them all to the party.
5 I haven't seen him for ages.

42.1
1 Let's see who *finishes* these *exercises* first.
2 The bar *closes* when the last customer *leaves*.
3 Don't make *promises* you can't keep.
4 Nobody *uses* a typewriter nowadays, do they?
5 My dad's so tall that when he *reaches* his hand up he *touches* the ceiling.

42.2
1 Joyce and Mike *are* Dennis's *parents*. / Joyce and Mike *are* Dennis's *mother* and *father*.
2 Tom *is* Dennis's *brother*.
3 James and Joyce *are* Mr and Mrs Birch's *children*. / James and Joyce *are* Mr and Mrs Birch's *son and daughter*.
4 Dennis is George's *grandson*.
5 Joyce *is* Mike Jones's *wife*.

42.3
1 Charles's	7 The camera's *Charles's*.
2 Rose's	8 The jacket's *George's*.
3 Charles's	9 The shoes are *Jez's*.
4 George's	10 The skis are *Rose's*.
5 Jez's	11 The suitcase is *Jez's*
6 Jez's	12 The map's *Charles's*.

43.1
1 I watched an interesting film. ✓	5 I phoned the police. ✗
2 I watched the news. ✗	6 They helped me a lot. ✗
3 I walked to the end of the road. ✗	7 They asked a lot of questions. ✓
4 The car stopped in the middle of the road. ✓	8 It rained all day. ✓

43.2
1 They *played* very well.	5 I *listened* to the radio.
2 We *cleaned* all the rooms.	6 I *wanted* to have a word with you.
3 We always *cook* a big meal for the whole family.	7 They *arrive* early in the morning.
4 I *need* some help with the housework.	8 I never *missed* the lesson.

43.3
1 We usually *finished* before the others.	5 I *loved* the music in the film.
2 You *pronounce* my name wrong.	6 We *talked* for hours and hours.
3 I *added* a bit of onion to the recipe.	7 I *pass* your house on my way to work.
4 I *like* those people but they always *stay* too long.	8 They *lived* by the sea.

44.1
1 A: How about meeting on Tuesday or Thursday at one o'clock?

   B: I can come on **Tuesday**, but not before **two** o'clock.

2 A: Let's go to the beach and have a swim.

   B: Well, I'll come to the **beach** with you, but I'll probably just do some **sunbathing**.

3 A: Which shop are you talking about? Is it on the corner?

   B: Well, it isn't on the **corner**, exactly, but it's very **near** there.

4 A: When I was at school I was good at maths and physics.

   B: I was good at **maths**, but my best subject was **music**.

44.2 1 A: Maybe we could have dinner on Thursday or Friday?
   B: Well, I'm free on **Thursday**.
 2 A: Let's have a quick drink at the pub and then go somewhere to eat.
   B: Well, I've got time to go to the **pub** for half an hour.
 3 A: Are the shops open in the evenings and on Sundays?
   B: Well, I know they're open in the **evenings**.
 4 A: My favourite school subjects were history and geography.
   B: Really? I liked **geography** …

44.3 1 A: It's freezing today!
   B: It's pretty **cold**, yes, but it's good weather for walking, so let's **go**!
 2 A: Did you go to university in Europe?
   B: I didn't **study** there, no, I just travelled **around**.
 3 A: Did you come on the ferry?
   B: No, I like travelling by **sea**, but it takes too **long**.
 4 A: We've got plenty of time – we're leaving at four.
   B: That's the **departure** time, yes, but we have to be there by **three**.

44.4 1 A: Are the shops open at the weekend?
   B: I know they're open on **Saturdays**.
 2 A: What did you think of the band?
   B: The **singer** was good.
 3 A: Have you been sightseeing yet?
   B: We've been to the **castle** – that's all we had **time** for today.
 4 A: Can I have something non-alcoholic?
   B: We've got some **orange** juice … or some **mineral water** …

There is no Key for Unit 45.

46.1 1 A: I was lying in **bed** last night, round about **midnight**, and I heard a knock at the **door**.
   B: *Oh? What did you do?*
   A: **Well**, I went **downstairs** …
 2 A: I was waiting for the **bus** yesterday, as **usual**, and **suddenly** I heard an **explosion**.
   B: *Did you?*
   A: **Yes**, and I thought What's **that**!?
 3 A: I was watching the **news** one night, and **suddenly** I saw **myself** in the **shopping** centre.
   B: *Sorry?*
   A: I said I saw **myself**, on **TV**!
   B: *That's amazing!*
 4 A: I left my **wallet** on the bus today!
   B: Oh, **no**! *That's terrible!*
 5 A: **Today** was **awful**!
   B: **Why**? *What happened?*
   A: **Well**, first the **bus** was late, then …
 6 A: I was walking by the **river** one day last **week**, down near the **bridge**, you **know**?
   B: *Yes?*
   A: And I heard a sort of loud **noise** in the **water** …

46.2   A: I was lying in **bed** last night, round about **midnight**, and I heard a knock at the **door**.

B: **Oh?** *Did you?*

A: **Yes**, and I thought, 'That's **unusual**.'

B: What did you **do**?

A: **Well**, I went downstairs, and looked through the **window**, and it was **dark**, of **course**, but I could see a **bus** in the street, with its **lights** off and no **passengers**, and a **man** standing at my door, with a sort of official-looking **cap** on his head.

B: *Sorry?*

A: A **cap**, you **know**, like **bus** drivers wear.

B: **Oh, I see**. *What happened?*

A: **Well**, I opened the **door**, and he said, 'Mr **Johnson**?', and I said, '**Yes**?' And he said, 'Here's your **wallet**. I finished **work** at **midnight** and I **found** it on my **bus**.' What do you think about **that**?

B: That's *amazing*!

47.1   1   A: How was the match?

       B: The first half was **quite** good, but the second half was **really** good.

   2   A: How was the match?

       B: The first half was quite **good**, but the second half was **terrible**.

   3   A: Can I come and discuss this tomorrow?

       B: **I** won't be here tomorrow, but my **colleague** will be.

   4   A: Can I come and discuss this tomorrow?

       B: I won't be here **tomorrow**, but I'll be back on **Thursday**.

   5   A: Have you seen that film?

       B: I've **seen** it, but I can't **remember** much about it.

   6   A: Have you seen that film?

       B: I **haven't** seen it, but I'd **like** to.

   7   A: Are you having trouble?

       B: I know what this word **means**, but I don't know how to **pronounce** it.

   8   A: Are you having trouble?

       B: I know what **this** word means, but I don't know any of the **others**!

   9   A: What did you think?

       B: I **liked** the film, but I didn't really **understand** it.

  10   A: What did you think?

       B: I liked the **film**, but the **seats** were so uncomfortable!

  11   A: I'd like to go to Britain to study for a month or two – or maybe even a year!

       B: I'd like to go to Britain for a **month**, but not for a **year**.

  12   A: I'd like to go to Britain to study for a month or two – or maybe even a year!

       B: I'd like to go to **Britain**, but I'd rather go to **America**.

47.2 1 A: What's the answer – three hundred and eighty-five?

B: No – three hundred and **ninety**-five.

2 A: After you.

B: No – after **you**.

3 A: You went to the disco with Steve last night, didn't you?

B: I didn't **go** with him – I **met** him there.

4 A: Do you live in London?

B: Well, not really **in** London, just **outside**.

5 A: You said go over the bridge.

B: No, I said go **under** the bridge.

6 A: Were there really fifty people at your birthday party?

B: Well, **nearly** fifty, I think.

7 A: What's 'Thank you' in Italian?

B: I can't **speak** Italian.

8 A: How many times have you been to England?

B: I've **never** been to England.

9 A: Was the course expensive?

B: Well, my school paid for the **course**, but the **travel** cost quite a lot.

10 A: How much should I bring – fifty pounds?

B: You'll need at **least** fifty.

48.1 1 A: Do you like westerns?

B: **Me**? I can't **stand** westerns!

2 A: It's stopped raining.

B: **Really**? I don't **believe** it!

3 A: Is it the first time you've been here?

B: The **first** – and probably the **last**!

4 A: You know the city pretty well, don't you?

B: **Me**? I've never **been** here before!

5 A: What are twelve elevens?

B: Don't ask **me**! I'm **hopeless** with numbers!

6 A: It's two pounds fifty for a cup of coffee.

B: **Two fifty**? That's **ridiculous**!

7 A: Were the shops busy today?

B: **Busy**? They were almost **empty**!

8 A: Do you like rap music?

B: **Like** it? I think it's **awful**!

49.2 1 A: Can I **help** you?

B: **No**, thanks, I'm just **looking**.

2 B: I'll take **this**, **please**.

A: **Sure**. Anything **else**?

B: **No**, thanks, that's all.

3 A: That's fifteen **forty** altogether.

B: **Here** you **are**.

4 A: Here's your **change**.

B: Thank **you**.

5 A: **See** you.

B: **Bye**.

49.3 A: Excuse **me**?

B: **Yes**?

A: Can you tell me the way to the **station, please**?

B: **Yes**, you just go along this **road**, cross the **bridge** over the **river** and there's a big **park** on your **left**, you **know**? **Well**, you go through the **park** and the **station's** just on the other **side**.

A: Is it **far**?

B: **No**, not **very** far.

A: **OK**, so I go along this **road**, cross the **bridge** and through the **park** – **right**?

B: That's **right**.

A: Thanks very **much**.

B: You're **welcome**. **Bye**.

A: **Bye**.

49.4 A: All **right**?

B: **Yes**.

A: Not **nervous**?

B: A **bit**.

A: Don't **worry**. It'll be **fine**.

B: I **hope** so.

A: **Right**. Let's **start**. Are you **ready**?

B: I **think** so.

A: **OK**. The first question **is** ... What's your **name**?

B: My **name**? ... It's ... Jack **Johnson**.

A: That's **right**! Well **done**! **Difficult**?

B: **Well**, not **too** bad.

A: **Right**. The **second** question is ... What's 37,548 × 7,726?

B: **What**!

50.2

it was!	usually
of course!	is it?
definitely	maybe
	really?
	I think so
	did you?
	sometimes

50.3

That's **great**!	That's **strange**.
That's **fantastic**!	That's **interesting**.
That's **marvellous**!	That's **good news**!
	That's **kind** of you!
	That's a **good idea**.

E3 Sound pairs

Sound pair 1

1 leave — live
2 live — live
3 feel — fill
4 fill — feel
5 filled — field
6 field — field
7 Tim — team
8 seat
9 will
10 eat
11 cheap
12 litter

Sound pair 2

1 near — knee
2 near — knee
3 B — beer
4 beer — beer
5 D — dear
6 dear — D
7 E — E
8 cheers
9 near
10 we
11 D
12 here

Sound pair 3

1 sit — sit
2 set — sit
3 lift — left
4 left — lift
5 litter — litter
6 letter — letter
7 lesson — listen
8 F
9 six
10 N
11 fill
12 desk

Sound pair 4

1 /uː/ — /uː/
2 /uː/ — /ʊ/
3 pull — pool
4 pull — pool
5 fool — full
6 full — full
7 look — Luke
8 /ʊ/
9 /uː/
10 pull
11 pull
12 fool

Sound pair 5

1 /ʊ/ — /ʌ/
2 /ʊ/ — /ʊ/
3 luck — look
4 look — look
5 look — luck
6 book — book
7 book — buck
8 /ʌ/
9 /ʊ/
10 look
11 look
12 book

Sound pair 6

1 boot — boat
2 boat — boot
3 soap — soup
4 soup — soap
5 show — show
6 shoe — show
7 throw — through
8 toe
9 grew
10 blue
11 boots
12 shows

Sound pair 7

1 hat	heart
2 heart	heart
3 March	match
4 match	March
5 park	park
6 pack	park
7 had	hard
8 heart	
9 match	
10 park	
11 hard	
12 had	

Sound pair 8

1 far	four
2 far	four
3 are	are
4 or	or
5 farm	form
6 form	farm
7 star	store
8 four	
9 or	
10 R	
11 port	
12 store	

Sound pair 9

1 cut	cat
2 cut	cut
3 cap	cap
4 cup	cap
5 match	match
6 match	much
7 ran	run
8 much	
9 match	
10 run	
11 sang	
12 rung	

Sound pair 10

1 lock	lock
2 luck	lock
3 not	not
4 nut	nut
5 gone	gun
6 gun	gone
7 shut	shot
8 lock	
9 box	
10 rung	
11 bus	
12 song	

Sound pair 11

1 /ɒ/	/əʊ/
2 /əʊ/	/əʊ/
3 not	not
4 coast	cost
5 want	want
6 note	
7 cost	
8 want	

Sound pair 12

1 or	oh
2 oh	or
3 caught	caught
4 coat	caught
5 walk	walk
6 so	saw
7 so	so
8 oh	
9 ball	
10 caught	
11 bought	
12 cold	

Sound pair 13

1 /ɒ/   /ɒ/
2 /ɒ/   /ɔː/
3 shot   short
4 pot   port
5 spot   spot
6 short
7 pot
8 sport

Sound pair 14

1 work   work
2 walk   work
3 saw   sir
4 saw   saw
5 born   born
6 born   burn
7 shirt   short
8 walk
9 burn
10 shirt
11 bird
12 walked

Sound pair 15

1 man   men
2 men   man
3 had   had
4 had   head
5 said   sad
6 sad   sad
7 pen   pen
8 men
9 sad
10 mat
11 set
12 bed

Sound pair 16

1 paper   pepper
2 pepper   paper
3 gate   gate
4 get   gate
5 wet   wait
6 wait   wet
7 late   late
8 pen
9 main
10 later
11 pepper
12 age

Sound pair 17

1 head   heard
2 heard   heard
3 bed   bird
4 bed   bird
5 turn   ten
6 turn   turn
7 went   weren't
8 bed
9 turn
10 weren't
11 worst
12 lend

Sound pair 18

1 /ʌ/   /e/
2 better   better
3 butter   better
4 one   when
5 again   a gun
6 better
7 one
8 nut

Sound pair 19

1 /ɜː/   /æ/
2 hat   hat
3 hat   hurt
4 bad   bird
5 heard   heard
6 hurt
7 bird
8 heard

Sound pair 20

1 /ɜː/   /ɪə/
2 beard   beard
3 bird   beard
4 here   here
5 we're   were
6 beard
7 her
8 were

Sound pair 21

1 wear	way
2 way	wear
3 A	A
4 A	air
5 stay	stair
6 stair	stay
7 hey!	hair
8 stair	
9 hair	
10 there	
11 K	
12 no way	

Sound pair 22

1 May	May
2 my	May
3 why	why
4 way	why
5 day	die
6 die	die
7 A	I
8 I	
9 white	
10 lake	
11 buy	
12 high	

Sound pair 23

1 pears	pears
2 bears	pears
3 pay	bay
4 bay	pay
5 pen	pen
6 Ben	Ben
7 B	P
8 pay	
9 Ben	
10 B	
11 buy	
12 pack	

Sound pair 24

1 fair	pear
2 pear	fair
3 full	full
4 full	pull
5 past	fast
6 fast	fast
7 coffee	copy
8 pear	
9 full	
10 past	
11 feet	
12 coffee	

Sound pair 25

1 watch	watch
2 what's	watch
3 toes	toes
4 chose	toes
5 test	chest
6 chest	chest
7 coats	coach
8 chose	
9 coat	
10 beach	
11 each	
12 eats	

Sound pair 26

1 try	dry
2 die	tie
3 die	die
4 down	down
5 town	down
6 white	wide
7 wide	wide
8 writing	
9 two	
10 D	
11 road	
12 said	

Sound pair 27

1	taught	thought
2	taught	taught
3	three	tree
4	three	three
5	boat	both
6	both	boat
7	mats	maths
8	taught	
9	thought	
10	three	
11	boat	
12	mats	

Sound pair 28

1	gold	cold
2	gold	gold
3	back	back
4	bag	back
5	class	glass
6	glass	glass
7	docks	docks
8	cold	
9	bag	
10	glass	
11	class	
12	dogs	

Sound pair 29

1	view	few
2	few	few
3	leaf	leave
4	leave	leave
5	very	ferry
6	ferry	ferry
7	lift	lift
8	view	
9	leaf	
10	very	
11	safe	
12	lived	

Sound pair 30

1	sing	thing
2	sing	thing
3	thought	thought
4	sort	thought
5	thick	sick
6	sick	thick
7	mouth	mouse
8	sing	
9	thought	
10	thick	
11	thumb	
12	mouse	

Sound pair 31

1	plays	plays
2	plays	place
3	Sue	zoo
4	zoo	zoo
5	ice	ice
6	eyes	eyes
7	rise	rise
8	place	
9	zoo	
10	niece	
11	peas	
12	eyes	

Sound pair 32

1	so	show
2	show	so
3	sheet	seat
4	seat	seat
5	short	short
6	sort	short
7	Sue	shoe
8	show	
9	sheet	
10	suit	
11	save	
12	shine	

Sound pair 33

1 shoes — choose
2 shoes — shoes
3 chip — chip
4 ship — chip
5 catch — cash
6 catch — cash
7 wash — wash
8 shoes
9 chair
10 cheap
11 catch
12 watch

Sound pair 34

1 ran — rang
2 ran — rang
3 thing — thin
4 thin — thin
5 thing — thing
6 think — thing
7 sink — sing
8 ran
9 thin
10 think
11 sing
12 sung

Sound pair 35

1 night — might
2 might — might
3 me — knee
4 knee — me
5 sun — sun
6 some — sun
7 some — sung
8 night
9 mice
10 nine
11 sung
12 swim

Sound pair 36

1 light — light
2 light — right
3 long — wrong
4 wrong — wrong
5 collect — collect
6 collect — correct
7 reader — leader
8 light
9 long
10 rock
11 correct
12 arrive

Sound pair 37

1 A — hey!
2 hey! — A
3 hear — hear
4 ear — ear
5 eye — eye
6 high — high
7 air — hair
8 A
9 heating
10 old
11 eight
12 heart

E5 The alphabet

E5.1
b	bee
c	see
i	eye
o	oh
p	pea
q	queue
r	are
t	tea
u	you
y	why

E5.2   1 w   2 j   3 y

E5.3   1 l   2 j   3 x   4 f   5 z   6 b   7 q   8 d   9 t   10 k   11 h   12 p

E5.4
1 bird	2 use	3 years	4 sixty	5 choose	6 key
7 guess	8 wait	9 jar	10 cheque	11 wave	12 edge

E6 Pronouncing numbers

E6.1
1 106
2 918
3 11,690
4 4,004
5 350,000

E6.2
1 1540
2 1603
3 1800
4 1945
5 2003

E6.3
1 0378 464 952
2 0208 56 77 82 03
3 01446 847 392
4 0048 57 766 5412
5 0500 2875 9104

E6.4
1 32°
2 −11°
3 August 20th / 20 August
4 21st
5 $5\frac{3}{4}$
6 1.6093
7 67.7%
8 $\frac{2}{3}$

E8 Homophones

1 *Bye* for now. / What did you *buy*?
2 *Write* your name. / That's *right*.
3 I can't *see*. / The deep blue *sea*.
4 When shall we *meet*? / Do you eat *meat*?
5 *Check* the answers. / Pay by *cheque*.
6 I don't know what to *wear*. / *Where* are you?
7 I don't *know*. / *No*, I don't.
8 Come *here*. / I can't *hear* you.
9 Our *new* house. / I *knew* the answer.
10 I feel *weak*. / The end of the *week*.

Acknowledgements

I would like to thank Frances Amrani for commissioning and guiding the project and Alison Silver for her assiduous and supportive editorial work.

I would also like to thank the following reviewers for their feedback on the first version of the manuscript:
Melanie Bell, Cambridge, UK
Barbara Bradford, Kent, UK
David Hill, Sydney, Australia
Jean Meakin, Buckinghamshire, UK
Gillian Paterson, Paris, France

The IATEFL Pronunciation Special Interest Group (PronSIG) has been a constant source of inspiration and opportunity for experimentation over the past 20 years (see www.iatefl.org).

Jonathan Marks 2007

James Richardson produced the audio recordings at Studio AVP, London.

Illustrations by Jo Blake, Mark Draisey, Julian Mosedale and David Shenton

Cover design by Dale Tomlinson

Designed and typeset by Kamae Design, Oxford